Group Captain LEONARD CHESHIRE, v.c.,
d.s.o., d.f.c., has become a legend in his own
lifetime. He took part in many dangerous
bombing raids on German cities; he was an
official British observer when the atomic bomb
was dropped on Nagasaki, in 1945. After the
war, he turned to more peaceful, philanthropic
activities. He was a founder of the Cheshire
Foundation Homes for the Sick, and a
co-founder of the Mission for the Relief of
Suffering.

Bomber Pilot

Leonard Cheshire, V.C., D.S.O., D.F.C.

Mayflower

Granada Publishing Limited
Published in 1975 by Mayflower Books Ltd
Frogmore, St Albans, Herts AL2 2NF

First published in Great Britain by
Hutchinson & Co Ltd 1943
Copyright © Leonard Cheshire 1943
Made and printed in Great Britain by
Cox & Wyman Ltd
London, Reading and Fakenham
Set in Monotype Garamond

GLOSSARY

Astro	Navigation by the stars.
Bearing	Usually a wireless aid to navigation indicating a position line from the point of origin.
C.S.C.	A mechanical computer for applying wind speed and direction to the course to steer.
Cumulonimbus	A type of cloud, commonly called 'heap' or billow cloud.
D.R.	Dead reckoning. A process of ascertaining one's position in the air without being able to verify it by map reading.
E.T.A.	Estimated time of arrival. 'E.T.A. the coast' means estimated time of arrival at the coast.
Fix	A position on the map plotted by wireless.
F.T.S.	Flying Training School.
Glycol	A coolant liquid used instead of water because of its resistance to cold.
Intercom.	Telephone system inside an aircraft.
Met.	Meteorological Section.
Perspex	Transparent wind-shield.
R/T	Radio telephony.
U.S.	Unserviceable.
W/T	Wireless – morse, not speech.

LIST OF ILLUSTRATIONS

(All photographs appear by courtesy of the Imperial War Museum)

CHAPTER ONE

INITIATION

Nine o'clock in the morning, June 1940: a crew room somewhere in Yorkshire. I am still feeling my way; everything is
new and interesting, even the smallest detail. Faces round
about are strange; I feel rather self-conscious, almost apolo-
getic – they are seasoned fighters, I am a new boy; at least,
that is how I feel. Some of the faces are familiar, though –
Frammy, Lousy and Lofty. Yes, Lofty, he is the captain of
my crew. I only met him yesterday, but yesterday was a fateful day: I was put down to fly with Masham, but at half past
four in the afternoon it was changed, and now Masham is
dead, with all his crew. I was lucky. Lofty gives you confidence; he is tall and strong and bronzed; comes from New
Zealand. He has a sort of devil-may-care look and I don't
think he gives a damn about anybody, however exalted they
may be. He won a D.F.C.; almost the first of the War.

The Flight Commander came in, tubby and jovial; just the
opposite of Lofty, but he scares you a bit. He read out roll-
call. As he was doing it I tried to catch people's names and
connect them with faces, but I found it too difficult and gave
it up. He read out two letters, the first from the C.-in-C.
Bomber Command, the second something about air firing
regulations – I didn't quite understand it. Then he read the
crew list for tonight – Rex, Frammy, Lofty. Yes, definitely
Lofty. What a wonderful sound, too! My heart leapt, and my
face must have shown it, for Lofty winked. A few more
words about general topics and the Flight Commander went
out.

I had not had much chance to get together with Lofty, so
he took me into the Navigation Office and put me through a
cross-examination to see what I knew. He asked me about
my flying; whether I was any good on instruments.

9

'Fourteen hours night; 380 day.'

'Well, we'll have to make do on that.'

Then he asked me about the Whitley: what speed to fly at, engine revolutions, boost, bomb-loads. Explained why you cruise fast when you are heavily loaded and slower when you are light, when to use weak mixture, what height to put in high-speed supercharger. Asked me whether I knew about the guns, how to clear a stoppage, how to work the turret; bombs, selector switches. If I knew how to use 'Mickey Mouse', to open and shut bomb-doors, or use a bomb-sight without hitting something two miles away from the target. Petrol cocks, endurance ranges, engine temperature and pressures – everything under the sun, till I didn't know whether I was coming or going. Then we went on to crew drill. We imagined we were going down in the sea and had to get out into the dinghy – I didn't quite know how to unhook the dinghy so we went in an aircraft and tried it out; also what position to take up to resist the impact on hitting the water.

We worked out, too, the best way to jump if ever we should have to. Then he ran briefly over navigation and wireless procedure. Did I know what we did to identify ourselves as friendly, and when or if you were lost how to ask for a fix or a homing bearing, and under what circumstances you could use them? What frequencies and wavebands were available, what form you should send a message in and when you should keep wireless silence. Letters and colours of the day, also; where they were kept and when they were used. He talked about evasive action, about guns and searchlights, what height to fly at, how long you can fly straight and level and still keep a margin of safety. I wanted to ask him about some of his trips, how he won his D.F.C., what it felt like to be fired at, but there wasn't time, so I kept quiet.

I was for the time being a second pilot; over enemy territory I would not be doing much flying, so it was my job to keep a look-out and note anything out of the ordinary. He told me of the sort of things Intelligence Branch would want to know: how to differentiate between fires on the ground and flares in the air. Roughly, how to tell the size of a ship, how also to see the bomb-bursts. He asked me if I had all my flying clothing and suggested what to wear and what not to wear. A lot of other things, too. How to change over seats, to let go of everything and jump out as quickly as possible, not to hold on to the stick while the other man was getting in; you only got confused that way. Could I map-read – had I ever tried it at night? Could I work out a course for home so that the navigator would not have to do it after he had dropped the bombs and so waste time? He said we were partners, he did not propose to do anything or make a decision without discussing it first. He chucked me under the chin and smiled, and then we went out to our aircraft.

Its letter was 'Q' – 'Q' for Queenie. The wireless operator and the gunner and the ground crew were out there already. The guns had been harmonized, but their action had not been checked. We put the ammunition tanks in, fed the rounds up to the guns and cocked them once or twice to see that they were not jamming in the chute. They seemed to be working perfectly, but I didn't really know much about it. The turret was hydraulic; we tested it for rotation, depression and elevation and saw that it was free of air. The perspex had to be cleaned, too, but that was the ground crew's job, and they had done it already. The wireless operator had finished his D.I. by now. He reported the set was O.K., that the intercom was working clearly and that there were no shorts or deficiencies in the electrical circuits. It was 12.20. Lofty had a few words with the sergeant in charge of the ground crew and we took off for a short flight to see there was nothing wrong. When we landed, the armourers were standing by to bomb up, sitting on the long caterpillar trailers that carried the bombs.

After lunch I went to bed. There was a maze of details running through my mind which I could not seem to sort out. I had figured out you more or less got into the plane, took off, dropped your bombs and came back, and that was that. I seemed to be learning. The night before I had been to town. Frammy was to have picked me up at midnight, but he did not turn up, and I had to walk back. They told me it was only six miles, but it turned out to be seventeen, and the walk took me all night, so now I went to sleep almost at once. The batman came in at 4.30. I went over to tea, had two eggs, and walked over to Headquarters for briefing.

The meteorological expert was the first on the list. He had with him a large complicated chart covered with lines and curves and curious markings which he proceeded to explain, but his explanation did not mean much to me and I was forced to fall back on his general description at the end. As far as I could gather, there would be broken cloud all the way: more or less clearing over the target but thickening and lowering on return. Then came the Intelligence Officer. He talked briefly about the position of the battle front, about the German advance and where they had reached, or, rather, where he thought they had reached, because nobody seemed quite to know. On the large map on the wall was a red line; they called it the bombline, and it was supposed to represent the area behind which we could bomb; beyond it we would be bombing our own troops. He told us why we were doing this trip – it was Abbeville, the southern bridge. We were to help hold up the German advance by destroying his lines of communication. He made us feel the plight of such British troops as were left in France, and, if nothing else, he succeeded in instilling in us the will to succeed.

Then he became more technical; told us how a bridge could be destroyed; the bomb must fall very close, close enough to blow up one of the supports, or else score a direct hit and explode instantaneously. He told us, too, what angle of approach to make so as to give maximum chance of being successful. Landmarks, too. At Abbeville it was comparatively easy; there was the River Somme with its mouth at Le Crotoy. Then something about opposition. The Germans had not been in Abbeville long; they could not have brought many guns with them – perhaps a few light Bofors type, but nothing heavy. Of troop concentrations he knew nothing – he hoped perhaps we might see some, and if not attack them be able to report them. Shipping we were to leave strictly alone. There were too many of our ships in the neighbourhood, and we could not hope to distinguish them by night. He ended up with hours of twilight.

The Signals Officer said a few words, but mostly for the

benefit of wireless operators. He ran through the frequencies and D.F. stations available, and emphasized the identification procedure. Then came the C.O. He gave us our recommended bombing heights. In view of the opposition expected we were to go in low. We were to drop all the bombs in one stick at thirty-yard intervals; better that way than in two small sticks. There were to be a lot of aircraft at the same time over the same place, therefore we were all to carry out left-hand circuits so as to avoid the danger of collision. He gave us times of take-off: one-minute intervals. Lofty was third off. On the return journey we were to take particular care to avoid London and all defended areas; in other words, since we were flying up England from the south we were not to cross the coast until we were certain where we were. We were to attack the target and then come straight back, not to fly around looking for Germans. Half our job was to drop the bombs in the right place, the other half to get back intact and fit to fly again. Then navigation: to make use of all available aids; to check the 'met' winds by visual pin-point if possible: if not, by taking drifts or Astro sights, or in the last resort by W/T. He said we were to expect to maintain maximum effort for some days, therefore we were not to waste time, but sleep and rest as soon as possible. He wished us good luck, and we went up to the hangars to make out the flight plan.

Percy, our navigator, Lofty and myself were there in the Navigation Office. The track was easy; we did not have to work out which was the best route to take, for it had been given us: Base, Abingdon, Eastbourne, Abbeville and back the same way. Percy laid it off on the chart: amazingly neatly, too. I was most surprised and impressed; he did not look as though he would be neat, but none the less he was. He measured off the distances and the bearings and filled in the log. Then we sorted out the navigational equipment and stowed it in the satchel. I never knew there could be so much stuff for what I imagined was a simple operation. Maps, rulers, compass, dividers, C.S.C., pencils, rubber, penknife, code books, computer, plotter, Astro tables, watch, sextant, planisphere, protractor, log book and Very cartridges. Percy seemed to be quite happy about all this, so I took it he had the matter well in hand and went off to change and have supper.

Up to now there had been too much to do to have time to think, but those few moments of anticipation during supper were worth every minute of the frustration of nine months' training. Lofty gave me a beer and said:

'Here's to you, Cheddar.'

'Don't call me Cheddar.'

'Why not?'

'I'm not rationed.'

He laughed his quick laugh and we walked up to the hangars.

I barged into the Crew Room and thought of the one and only time I have ever been into a parrot-house. Never have I seen a crowd of people all in such high spirits at the same time. Confusion, too. Parachutes, harnesses, flying suits, navigation bags, everything scattered all over the floor as well as the table, without regard for anybody. People were rushing around shouting at the top of their voices; how anybody knew what the others were saying God alone knows. Rations were spread anywhere; people filling their pockets with what they wanted – mostly chewing gum, chocolate and gum-drops as far as I could see – and giving the rest to their navigator to keep in his satchel. I put the stuff in an empty corner, but before I had got my sidcot on most of the rest were gone. I managed to find it eventually and checked it over. Boots, sidcot, helmet, gloves, scarf, harness, 'chute, oxygen tube and rations. Yes, it was all there, but I wasn't going to let it out of my sight again. Lofty came in, towering above everybody else; he wasn't difficult to pick out. He had been dressing in the Navigation Office – wiser than I. He kicked me on the bottom and told me to hurry up. He called the rest of the crew and we piled into a lorry standing outside. Percy told me to throw my kit in and jump on, but, thinking I would never see it again, I hung on to it for dear life. A few people standing on the tarmac smiled and put their thumbs up as we went past. I didn't recognize any of them, but smiled back. The lorry stopped with a jerk.

'"Q" for Queenie, anybody for "Q"?'

'Yes, wait a moment. Don't be in such a God-damned hurry.'

'See you in the morning, laddy.'

'O.K., Jimmy. All the best.'

Life was a bit easier now; room to move about in. It was five to eight – 35 minutes to go. The starter battery was in place and the ground crew were standing by; had been for the last hour. Lofty went over to the N.C.O. in charge and spoke to him. Percy looked the bombs over and started stowing his gear in the aircraft. I dumped my stuff on the ground and lay down to smoke a cigarette. An armourer came over to Percy, handed him the bomb-load chart and made him sign for the pins. Soon Lofty unhitched himself from the starter battery and swung into the aircraft. I threw my cigarette away and followed suit reluctantly – it is a job I hate doing. I am not as tall as Lofty, and the hatch being underneath the nose is on a level with my shoulders so that I have got to put my elbows on the floor of the aeroplane and hoist myself up. The only way not to fall out again is to wedge a knee against a corner of the hatch and get another handgrip, a procedure which to me at least is excessively painful, not to mention exhausting. However, I wriggled in somehow and settled down in the nose so as to be out of the way. I put my parachute and maps in the stowages, loaded the guns and plugged into the intercom to await developments. I always feel a bit shy talking down the intercom, rather like being on the stage unexpectedly. Still, I suppose I shall get used to it. The intercom seemed all right so I came back to the second pilot's position beside Lofty. It is not a position really; you sit on the floor and dangle your legs over the step, but you can see what is happening, and after a bit of wriggling about you seem more or less to fit in the corrugations.

Lofty opened the side window and shouted:

'O.K. for starting up?'

'O.K., sir.'

'Stand clear. Contact port engine.'

'Contact.'

The engine turned over once or twice, belched a mess of black smoke and roared into life. Lofty raised his right thumb and after a few turns the starboard motor started too. Followed a period of settling down and looking round. One by one the O.K.s came through from the rear gunner, the wireless operator and Percy. Then Lofty ran the engines up. He tested the petrol cocks, the magnetos, the airscrew pitch controls and the boost; opened the throttles fully, checked the revs and the boost and tested the magnetos again. He tried the bomb-doors and the flaps to see that they were working properly; looked at the trimmer tabs and set the compass and the gyro. The N.C.O. handed him the engine log; he signed it and shouted down the intercom:

'Stand by to take off.'

The final O.K. came from the crew. The chocks were waved away and we taxied out. I was glad I was not flying: I could not see which direction the wind sock was pointing, but Lofty didn't seem to have any difficulty; perhaps he had looked on the way up in the van. We reached the down-wind side of the aerodrome and looked at the time – two minutes to go. 'N' and 'P' were there before us; they waited a few moments, and when they had gone we turned into wind. Nothing coming; off we went.

We circled the aerodrome, gaining height. It was still broad daylight and I could see the men and women standing around, looking up at us and waving; some of them even got off their bicycles to do it. I smiled, and thought: 'You don't know how much that means to me; it is the first time a complete stranger has ever waved and wished me good luck.' I stopped looking at them and went into the front turret to try to get to know it better. I shut my eyes to see if I could find everything in the dark – intercom plug, oxygen point, ammunition pans. Percy shouted out the first course; Lofty checked it back and set it on the compass. I lay in the turret looking at the ground. It seemed to mean more than it usually does. I noticed more details; wondered what people in the houses would be doing – going to bed, perhaps. No, I suppose not; too early. But anyway, their work was over, ours more or less starting. They would be having dinner maybe, or sitting around smoking and chatting, thinking they had done a good day's work and earned their rest. I didn't envy them.

Curious remembrances and thoughts came back to me: parked outside a pub I could see a lot of cars. I had done that so often myself, but what a wonderful thing for once to have an evening's entertainment provided for you and to know at the same time you are actually going to do somebody some good. I thought, too, of the evenings I had said, 'What the hell am I going to do to amuse myself tonight?' and it occurred to me that you do not appreciate the simple things in life until you suddenly realize you may never encounter them again. My mind went back to the people in the pub; they could probably hear the noise of our engines and wonder idly what we were doing. They would think of us as a mechanical entity, not as a vehicle containing five ordinary humans, thinking the same sort of thoughts as they were.

We were a bit higher now, 3,000 feet. It was getting darker; I could not see details quite so well, but everything looked peaceful. Felt happy and sleepy – well, not sleepy, just dreamy. The steady drone of the engines makes you that way. I was quite happy to sit still and have things done for me instead of having to do them myself. Something woke me: it was Lofty.

'Come and take over, Cheddar. Let's see what your flying is like before it gets dark.'

'O.K.'

I unplugged the intercom lead and put the end in my pocket; it is on a long flex and trips you up if you don't do that. Switched the lights off, looked round to see I hadn't forgotten anything and wriggled out. On the floor of the well is the door; it gave me a prickly feeling that it might collapse if I trod on it, so very gingerly I avoided it. In pulling myself up I missed the handle and covered my hands with grease from the rudder-bar. Lofty waited till he had the aircraft flying straight and level, looked at me to see if I was ready, and suddenly darted out of his seat. I would not have believed he could be so agile. My efforts to rival him were unsuccessful. I knocked the undercarriage lever down and threw the aircraft 20° off course. He made a rude sign and I settled down to concentrate on flying. Percy moved forward to the front turret and started to map-read. I think he must have got some pin-points, for he managed to work out a new wind. He gave me an alteration of course, and a few moments later he handed up our E.T.A. to Abingdon. From the way he kept peering over my shoulder at the compass and air-speed indicator I gathered he did not trust my flying. It made me nervous, even though he was a sergeant, and to add to that I could not quite remember what engine revs and boost I had been told to fly at, so I left them as they were. From time to time I had to change the throttle opening just enough to maintain the correct air speed, that was all. The engines kept de-synchronizing, which gave a sort of alternating irritating drum, but Lofty dealt with that so that I could concentrate on flying.

As the minutes ticked by it grew darker and darker. I began to feel restless: moved in my seat, shook my head and blinked. Percy said E.T.A. was up in ten minutes. I felt worried in case my course had been inaccurate, but I had no map and didn't know where we were. I tried to gain consolation from Percy's expression, but could only see the back of his head. Then suddenly he came out: he raised his thumb and beamed. It must be all right. Lofty had disappeared: he must have gone somewhere down the fuselage. I looked out of the window; the light was failing and I had to get my eyes accustomed. The exhaust flames just to the left were beginning to get bright and blinded me; but I knew the country like the back of my hand; after all, I had lived in it for 22 years, all my life. The first thing I recognized was the aerodrome. The tarmac and hangars were quite clear now I knew what to look for. Yes, everything was falling into place, just like a jigsaw puzzle. The quarry and Cothill School right beneath us. Well, I'd missed Oxford; that must be seven miles behind us now; no matter, but I should have liked to have seen it none the less. Merton College especially, with its tower and its chimes. Three years I'd been there studying law. The Air Force was the life I had wanted, not law – freedom of the skies and no brainwork, but much as I had wanted to be rid of

Oxford I had benefited from it. Thank God Father had insisted I go. I thought of the library where Jack and Douglas and I had worked so often. Someone was probably still working there now. The Dons would be sitting round in the Common Room drinking their port. I wondered what subject they were discussing – probably the war. Their usual subjects would have been relegated to second place now. Isn't that funny? – if I were there I could meet them for the first time in my life on ground I knew better than they. I almost saw them standing round with gaping jaws hanging on my every word, but it was only a passing vision: they had long forgotten me now. I was just another mediocre pupil who had laughed and idled his way through three years. Percy's voice woke me.

'147.'

'What about it?'

'New course.'

'Don't be in such a hurry.'

'We are past Abingdon: it's time to turn.'

'Shut up.'

The Marcham road was below. I could not see the trees or the woods very well, but the house I could, just. I strained to get a better view, but it didn't help much, so I pictured it in my mind: Father reading a book, Mother shutting the geese up – she must be right down below this very minute – whistling 'Clair de Lune' and possibly wondering what I am doing; but she does not know I'm here. I told her I wouldn't be flying for another week at least; better that way.

'What was that course, again?'

'147. 14 . . .'

'O.K. I've got it; 147. Pass it up on a slip if you like.'

He passed it up and came back to his table. He had found a new wind and checked it up, so map-reading for the time was not necessary, not till we reached the coast. He sat for a while writing and plotting; then he lay back and started chewing gum. Lofty woke him up; he wanted to get past, and as there was not room for both of them it meant Percy had to stand up and wedge himself between the navigation table and the back of my seat. He looked disapproving and Lofty seemed amused. I was amazed he had trusted me so long by myself. He checked over the instrument readings and told me to change over tanks. I did not quite like the idea, because I had to switch off the tank we had been using before switching on the other one in case of air locks, and I thought the engines might stop. Still, nothing seemed to happen. Lofty climbed down into the well and stood there with one foot on the step, gazing out of the starboard window. Occasionally he made some remark, asked me how I was getting on, and all the time he kept a close eye on the flying panel. Now and then when he saw a beacon or landmark he went back to Percy and plotted it on the chart. The wireless operator handed him a message; what it was I did not know. He pored over it for a time, picked up a book which he compared with the message and wrote something in the log. I asked Percy to dim his light; it reflected on the perspex in front and I couldn't see out.

'E.T.A. Eastbourne up in ten minutes.'

Percy went to the front turret again to map-read. Lofty map-read, too, out of the side window. I noticed the black-out; here and there was an occasional twinkle; cars I could see, too, if they had their headlights on, but nothing else. A few searchlights flickered on to us just long enough to see what we were, and then switched off.

Then I saw the coast. At first just a dim line; then it grew clearer, and as we got over it I saw a largish town. Percy shouted: 'Eastbourne.' How he knew I did not know; to me it seemed unrecognizable. Still, he had a map and I hadn't. I could see the shore quite clearly now: the breakers, too. Percy gave me a new course, I set it on the compass and headed out to sea. Yes, out to sea. Lofty nudged me; I got the plane flying straight and level, unhitched my intercom plug and jumped out, this time doing no damage. A search-light came on us from the shore as a sort of farewell message, and Lofty took over. I stood in the well for a few moments stretching myself and rubbing my backside. I had not been flying long, it is true, but I was not yet used to it. I ate a bis-cuit and climbed into the front turret to test the guns, which incidentally gave Lofty a shock; he was not expecting it, and thought the tracer was coming from somewhere else. I was feeling keyed up, like waiting for the curtain to go up. Below there was a mass of what looked like lights; I wondered what they were. Too many of them to be ships; no, they could not be ships, but, if not, what on earth were they? Then I realized they must be white horses. I visualized the evacuation of Dunkirk; some of the boats might still be down below us. The rear gunner came through on the wire; reported the turret O.K. Lofty climbed up a thousand feet and started talking to Percy, then suddenly I saw the French coast. I gazed at it fascinated, as though it were a snake from the Zoo. For nine months I had read of the war in the papers – that was my only contact, and now suddenly I was right on the scene. What struck me most was that it looked just like the English coast. No reason in the world why it should not, but then that is the way it is. Just a light-coloured line dividing sea from land. That was all, but the land it divided was the scene of the collapse of France. To port I could just see a bend; on looking closer I could see it was an estuary. We were just about there. I moved back and let Percy in to get ready for bombing. I wished him good luck, but he couldn't hear me above the roar of the engines, so I gave it up. The wireless operator was idly twiddling dials and looking bored; Lofty chewing gum.

'What do you want me to do?'

'Nothing. Just look around and get used to things.'

He seemed to spend most of his time looking out of the window, not at his instruments; it amazed me, yet his course was good.

Something flashed across the corner of my eye. I started, and looked around. There was nothing to be seen, yet I could have sworn I saw something. Over on the starboard a sort of orange pin-prick appeared. It grew steadily bigger, and then I saw it was a fire, then another; several more; the whole place seemed to be burning. They had told me it would be before we started, but I expected them to look so much larger. They were actually small. I could see no details; the river, just, but nothing else. Again something flashed across the corner of my eye. This time I just caught it; it was ground-to-ground tracer, firing east and so probably British. Perhaps anti-tank guns, who knows? I kept on looking and saw it was all over the place, but only desultory, not continuous. Perhaps they were tanks. A few tracer started coming up, not very close and very little of it, perhaps two or three guns. I thought: 'How slow they are going!' also 'How peculiar!' They would go straight for a time, and then, when they were right above us, start wavering about.

'When is E.T.A. up?'

'One minute. We are just about there.'

I could see the river but nothing else. 'It's too dark, we'll have to drop a flare.'

'O.K. Wireless op. . . . wireless op. What the hell's happened to him?'

'Just gone back; he won't be plugged in yet.'

'What the hell's that?'

'What's what?'

'Can't you see it – a great ball of flame just beside us?'

'Someone has just dropped a flare above us.'

'Is that it? I thought it was a gun, or shell, or something.'

'I think we are there; better drop a flare.'

'O.K. Wireless op?'

'Yes, sir; flare ready.'

'Let her go.'

'Flare gone, sir . . . do you want another one?'

'Yes, get the next one ready, same fuse setting, 3,000 feet.'

'Rear gunner, can you see anything? Has the flare gone yet?'

'No, not yet, Captain. Yes, there it is, it's burning O.K. I can't see the town, though.'

'O.K. I'll turn on to it and have a look.'

The intercom was new to me, it was an effort to hear; perhaps I was too interested looking around; anyway, I did not follow much more. Suddenly flares appeared all around us, dozens of them. They looked like orange balls, and it was difficult to tell whether they were on the ground or in the air, or what distance they were. I confused them with fires, and only when they were very close could I be certain; then they blinded me so that I could see nothing anyway. I expected the whole ground to be illuminated, but somehow it didn't seem to be. I became utterly confused; perhaps I spent too long staring at what was new to me. Lofty was circling steeply. I wondered how he could do it without watching his instruments, and felt frightened lest he should spin in. We dropped two more flares. The others seemed to know what they were doing, but I had lost all sense of direction – I could see even less than before. They were talking again now: something about fusing the bombs and opening the bomb-doors. Lofty was levelling out. I heard him say:

'Straight ahead; running up. It's right in front of you now. Can you see the river?'

'Yes, O.K., I've got it. There's the jetty. Wizard! Oh, wizard! The flare's right above the bridge. What's your heading?'

'170.'

'O.K. Left, left; left, left; no, further, much further. O.K., steady. Left, left; hold it; hold it. Christ, what was that?'

'Just another Whitley; only just missed us, though.'

'Left, left; steady; steady.'

'God Almighty!'

'What's the matter?'

'The bridge has gone.'

'What do you mean – it's gone?'

'It's been blown up. You never said "bombs gone".'

'It wasn't our bombs. It must have been someone else just ahead of us. Shall I bomb the northern bridge?'

'No, that's not our target; "B" flight are on that. We'll turn round and do another run-up. We'll have to drop another flare, though; it's gone out.'

'O.K. Wireless op. Wireless op.'

'Yes, sir; flare ready.'

'Hang on a moment . . .' and so round again we went. The same performance all over once more, only this time the bombs went. And found their mark.

Percy came out of the front turret; he looked pleased. Personally, I had not seen a thing; no bridge, no bombs. Lofty asked me how I'd enjoyed it. I was disappointed in a way, but, if nothing else, I felt happy from the infection of their high spirits. The rear gunner started talking; I'd almost forgotten he was there. Said he'd seen the bombs burst diagonally across the river, the first one on the starboard bank. He wasn't quite sure about the bridge, though, because he had not seen it; he'd seen other bombs from other aircraft, too. I saw some more ground-to-ground tracer, but nothing up at us. Percy was at his table again, writing furiously; wireless operator working away at his set. The French coast loomed up again; this time I saw a little more, the breakers and white horses stood out more clearly. I thought of the troops behind. I was going back to a warm bed and breakfast, but what had they to look forward to? Felt a curious sense of detachment: almost unreal, like being at a cinema. The coast came and went and I felt less detached. The sea was like a blanket; it looked so calm from above, but I suppose it was not.

Half-way across Lofty handed over to me again. I was expert at changing seats now. He hung around for a while, pulled some biscuits from his pocket and drank some coffee; then he kicked Percy out of his seat and struggled past him to Radley, the wireless operator. Radley was new: he seemed to be having difficulty in getting a message to Base, and Lofty went to help him. The clouds were filling up and lowering, so we never saw the English coast: but we turned on E.T.A. in spite of what the Wing Commander had said about making certain of our position, for we knew that at the worst we could not be far out. The tops of the clouds were 2,000 feet. I lost height a little and flew just above them. Overhead it was clear, clear as crystal. The stars stood out in their hosts. I love the stars; they are so friendly; wise, too. If ever you are in trouble, turn to the stars; they will give you the answer. Ahead there was a slight horizon from the clouds, so I did not have to fly on instruments all the time. There was a star silhouetted against the top right-hand corner of the panel. I leaned my head back and used it as a compass. As long as it stayed where it was we must be flying straight, and it was pleasant to stretch my neck instead of looking down all the time. Lofty must have thought I was going to sleep; he asked me what I was playing at; said he wanted to sit with the wireless operator and to let him know when I wanted a spell. I told him the more flying I did the happier I was, and he looked as though he thought I was mad.

The clouds began to break; it was still very dark and I could see no details. On the ground there were fewer lights and fewer cars than on our way out. But the searchlights showed great activity, though they must have been practising, for only one caught us. I moved about in my seat and Percy gave me a cup of coffee. Getting sore. Rear gunner must have been getting sore, too; he said:

'Must be about home now, aren't we, Captain?'

'Another hour yet.'

I gave up flying by the star and went back to instruments. Up above it grew lighter; the stars were fading. Well, I would be going to bed soon, too. Lofty asked me if I wanted a spell; I said I was O.K. and drank some more coffee. I noticed for the first time that the dawn is mauve and not grey; curious I had never realized that before. On the ground it grew lighter, too; things were beginning to appear – woods and trees and canals. We passed over a few factories, all of them working at top speed. The bright red flames of the exhausts grew weaker and I thought how amazing that engines could stand up to such heat for so long. Percy got out his maps and started map-reading once more, but from the side window, not from the turret. The clouds had almost gone, only an odd one here and there. My mind was in a whirl. I needed time to piece everything together; somehow it had not quite been what I expected; not enough glamour, and too much to learn.

Over on the starboard it was very light; the sun would be up before long. Percy said:

'Fifteen minutes to go.'

The flames had almost gone – a light orange colour; no longer red. I could see another Whitley a little way ahead of us, slightly above. Lofty came forward again, smiled down at me as though to say, 'Good show', and took over. Percy's navigation must have been good, and my course too, come to that. He had only given one alteration and three minutes before E.T.A. we came right over the aerodrome. Circled it once, and as the sun came over the eastern horizon we landed – six hours' flying to the second.

From a great height Lofty stroked the long black stubble on his smiling chin and said:
'You'll soon be a full-grown man, won't you, Cheddar?'
'I will if I have any more of these eggs and bacon.'
'You've got to work for them, though,' and he laughed.
'That's what I mean.'

CHAPTER TWO

AWAKENING

It is getting late as I write this. Perhaps my mind is beginning to wander, I do not know. Anyway, I see before me countless visions of the past month and a half. The Wing Commander had warned us to expect maximum effort, and so it was. Sometimes four nights out of five: always one out of three. I had my bacon and eggs, and I bruised my knee until it became impervious to bruises. Yes, visions: visions in their hosts. Percy in the Crew Room laying off tracks and sorting out maps: in his navigator's seat, talking of E.T.A.s and courses and winds. Lofty's head and shoulders sitting over the wheel, rigid as a rock, and hour after hour. Bacon and eggs and tea in the half-light of dawn, and Lofty with his inevitable bottle of beer. Lofty, too, somewhere, I cannot quite remember where, looking disgruntled.

And Axtell's answer – he is the rear gunner, I forgot to tell you. He has a girl friend in town and practically never says a word:

'Are we still over Germany?'

'No.'

'Well, we wouldn't be likely to see a sausage, would we?'

English coasts and Dutch coasts and German coasts coming and going, not once but often: sometimes in the brilliant light of the moon, sometimes lurking in the virginity of darkness. And in coasts such a wealth of meaning. If hostile, the expectancy of wondering whether it is the right landfall, the thrill of knowing at last the fight is on. And then, if friendly, the thought: 'God, *how* friendly?' Never shall I forget the warmth of those dawn receptions. One day, just out to sea, a bird escorted us home to the coast. I do not know what sort of a bird it was: I never shall know. I only know it was soft and fluffy and that it flew along just beside the port wing-tip.

At first I thought my eyes were playing tricks, but Percy saw it too. I noticed the incredulous look on his face as he watched it.

On the radio they are playing the 'Grand Canyon Suite'. Normally it brings to me a picture of donkeys racing through rocks and mountains and scrub, but this time I see a vision of two engines ever beside me: two long protruding noses, almost Jewish, but comforting – very comforting. Engines that never falter, and a roar that I hear in my ears long after we have landed. Many are the hours I have sat beside Lofty watching them: on the way out aggressive, like two eyes thrusting out into the night – evil, yes, definitely evil, but therein lies their attraction – and on the return laughing, exultant. They live, these engines, and are human just as you and I are. The music brings to me, too, a picture of the eternal trek of light and dark: of the night rolling slowly in from the east and chasing the sun over the western horizon, and then, to the sound of returning engines, giving place to the sun once more. Fleeting visions of small things. Entries in my log book: Mannheim, Essen, Emden, Kiel, Hamm, Gelsenkirchen, and many others. Of days off: drinking and dancing in town. One day Melvin and I went bathing. The sea was very cold and Melvin refused to go in. He was a rowing blue from Oxford and therefore used to the cold, but none the less he refused: perhaps he was shy of changing in the open. As I was dressing on the beach, trying to sort the sand out of my socks and toes, a little girl came up and said she would like to do it for me. She did it too, most carefully and tenderly, until there was not a grain left; and when I thanked her as best I could, she said: 'You're doing something for me: I would like to do something for you.' And a disgruntled Melvin saying: 'What about me?' Of personalities: the people I lived and worked with, and the gay, carefree atmosphere that went with them.

Other visions, not so fleeting, of tragedy. Tony, Braham, Roger and the rest, missing. Six weeks ago, just before I came up north to join the Squadron, Tony, Braham and myself had met at home and drank to the future. The war had seemed far off then, but now it was close. Of the first plane I saw shot down. We were approaching Aachen on the way to Mannheim. On the starboard, not far away, some searchlights were weaving and searching about in the sky. One moment they were searching, the next they were fixed rigid in a cone, and in the centre was a smallish, light-coloured object – a Whitley. The cone appeared to stay rigid, with the Whitley still in the middle, for perhaps two minutes, until a stream of orange tracer reared up from the ground. Up and up it went without ceasing, right into the apex of the cone, and then suddenly the small white light turned into an orange flame. Still the tracer came up, and very soon several more flames appeared. When eventually these all merged into one single, burning mass, the whole lot began to fall. Slowly at first, then faster and faster, and tracer pouring into it all the time, so that anyone still left alive could have no chance of jumping.

Then the ugliest vision of all. Andrew, the tall, blond, mad Irishman who crowded more laughter and more action into five weeks than anyone would have thought possible. He started off slowly, but worked up fast. The incendiaries caught fire just after he had taken off. They were in the bomb-racks and therefore inaccessible, but he managed to land somehow and put them out before any great damage was done. A little later a flare exploded in the flare-chute. As it happened, he was still over England and so escaped with his life, but even then there was not much margin to spare. The next week he was crossing the Channel when a fighter attacked him. His rear gunner only saw it at the last moment, after it had opened fire, and Andrew's first warning of what was happening was the sound of bullets ripping through the cockpit. The action, while it lasted, was short, but none the less furious. Some of the crew were injured and the aircraft was badly damaged, but the fighter went down in flames and Andrew carried on to the target. He should not have done, no doubt, but he did. He dropped his bombs in the right place, and literally with a few yards to spare regained the cliffs of Dover. People said he was looking for trouble, and gave him a D.F.C. But Andrew was not satisfied with looking for trouble in the skies. He resorted to the roads and an M.G., and because he was asking for it, ended by breaking the car up. Somehow he escaped himself. I can see him so clearly, laughing his wild laugh and afraid of neither man nor machine. One night he burst into the Trout. Someone started up on politics, and in the argument that followed Andrew's eyes turned slowly into red: at least so it seemed. In the end he took the Flight Commander by the neck and threatened to murder him if he tried any more to sing 'Danny Boy' out of tune. Whether or not it was the red eyes, I don't know, but the Flight Commander gave up trying. Sten, in spite of his broad Scots accent, had the only voice that Andrew would tolerate, but the next day Sten flew into a balloon and killed himself: so we heard 'Danny Boy' no longer.

Such was Andrew's character. He stood in awe of nothing, and nothing ever succeeded in shaking his spirit. But people said he was looking for trouble. Ten days later he was hit by a burst of 3·7s. He struggled back most of the way, but this time he did not succeed in reaching the coast. His wireless was working and we knew more or less where he was, a hundred miles out to sea. A Hudson found him after ten hours and set about patrolling him, but a Me.110 chased the Hudson away and machine-gunned the dinghy. That day and night he must have drifted far, for no one managed to find him again in spite of a full-scale search. At the end of the second day Command's hopes were low. Perhaps the dinghy had been sunk by the 110. On the third day they fell lower still but just before dusk he was found. The news went round the Squadron like wildfire, and with it went toast after toast to his rescue, but at daylight, when a launch arrived at the scene, there were only two left in the dinghy. We did not know that for three-and-a-half days they had been without food or water. The first man to die had said suddenly, 'I'm going to get a taxi,' and thrown himself overboard. The second was violent. They held him back for a while, but the time came when they could hold him back no longer, and so he went too. The third was the sanest of them all: said simply, 'I can't stand it any longer,' and followed the others. At dawn Andrew and the rear gunner were the only two left. The rear gunner had been injured on the head by the trailing aerial of the patrolling Hudson, but he survived. Andrew died on board the ship that picked him up. The very same day a policeman came round to the mess with a summons for dangerous driving.

Another of the same ilk was Beau: very tough and quite mad. He could drink a pint of beer in three seconds and hold his breath for a phenomenal time. We offered him a bottle of whisky if he held it for two-and-a-half minutes. We told him he had won after three-and-a-half, and, knowing nothing of the extra minute, he looked slightly pale and said: 'Gee, I must be out of training.' Once, because a girl said he could not do it, he carved her initials on the back of his hand with a lighted cigarette. The scars are there still, about an inch long. Early on in the war he ran out of petrol returning from a very distant target. Being still over Germany – at least, that is what he thought – he proceeded to prepare for an escape. One by one he ripped every imaginable instrument out of the aircraft – clocks, compasses, rations, water-bottles, first-aid kit, Very pistol – even the axe – and crammed them into his pockets, so that he was self-sufficient for at least a fifteen-day route march through any kind of opposition. How he managed to squeeze out of the escape hatch, God knows; but he did. On the way down someone started firing at him, and as soon as he landed he heard people running towards him, so he lay flat on his back and hoped they would not notice him. When they came closer he recognized their voices – French. They were soldiers, and were converging on him, shooting for all they were worth. With a whoop of excitement he leapt to his feet and revealed himself, but he was brandishing a hand-bearing compass, and the Frenchmen, apparently mistaking him for a German with a grenade, let out a cry of terror, dropped their rifles and raced away into the distance. When, some weeks later, Beau was shot down, we saw over Holland someone flashing the Squadron letters up at us, and so we knew that he was safe.

These, and countless others, were the visions that ran through my mind, but they were the trees, and only a few of them at that. The shape of the wood, at first unprepossessing in aspect and in extent huge, came before my eyes slowly like the calculated unveiling of a statue. When I left training-school I had pictured myself as a fully-groomed operational pilot wanting but a short experience of gunfire to be complete. I saw myself a leader of five men, a captain in whose hands rested the lives of a crew, and in a different sense the lives of many hundreds of Germans on the ground. At interrogation too:

'Did you find the target?'

'Certainly.'

'Did you hit it?'

'Naturally.'

It was a pretty picture, but as an illusion it did not last long, no longer than it took me to realize that bombing is technical, a matter of knowledge and experience, not of setting your jaw and rushing in. And when you have the knowledge and the experience, the crux of the issue is crew co-operation. To achieve it you have to lay the foundation of confidence: confidence in the crew partly, and partly confidence in yourself, but more than anything confidence in the captain. Personally, I would prefer to be a lone wolf, but since this is impossible I pray God I may see co-operation at its best. To see it there is only one way. You have got to be good, and they have got to know it, and they will only know it by results: for once you cannot bluff. It is not difficult, anyone can do it; merely a matter of working hard enough, but, as I said, you cannot bluff. I trust Lofty implicitly; I know what that trust is worth. It is worth working for.

First and foremost I had to learn to fly; learn, and then cast the thought of flying away into the background. Flying in itself is wholly unpredominant: to have a perfect pair of hands is important, but it is only a question of degree, not the end-all and be-all. Smooth landings do not affect the success of an operation; it is finding the right way to the right place that matters. In other words, flying must be subconscious. A soldier does not learn to walk or he would not be a soldier, but he learns to walk far and in the right direction. Lofty let me fly all I wanted, at first over the sea and over England, then, as I grew more experienced, over Germany, and once over the target itself. When I was not with Lofty I took an aircraft and flew myself, by day and sometimes by night as well. I practised flying relaxed till I found it no more tiring than sitting down. I learned to fly on instruments till it was no more tiring than reading a book. At the same time I settled down to learn the weapons I handled, what there was and where it was. I blindfolded myself and moved round the aeroplane until I could lay my hands on everything without the use of eyesight. I learned to load the guns, to clear stoppages, to set the bomb-sight, and what to do with the selector switches. I learned about engines, too: how to take care of them: their limitations and their possibilities. Once we had engine trouble over the North Sea. The oil temperature rose and the engine revolutions flickered. Lofty looked worried and asked me whether we ought to turn back. I realized then that this was a situation I could not meet. To turn back for no good reason is a crime, and anyway you will never persuade people you were not yellow: to carry on with no chance of return – suicidal: just as well to know, but I knew nothing about engines. For this I turned to the ground crews, and their anxiety to teach me was the greatest stimulus I could ever want.

With a fair understanding of all this I was ready for a crew. I could take off, cover the distance and land safely; but what is that? Flying and knowledge of the tools were the fundamental background, but no more than a background. At training-school, being ignorant, I used to indulge in fanciful visions. I saw myself roaring in low to the attack. I saw buildings and factories and ships blowing themselves sky-high, and trees rushing past the wing-tips, and, of course, to complete the picture, curtains of ack-ack all around. On June 9th, 1940, I saw myself on the threshold of putting these visions into fact. The only worry, and that was eclipsed by the excitement of operating at last, was gunfire. Suppose I was frightened; suppose I found myself to be a coward and cried out for mercy! It could be. No one else did that, but then that is no help. It is difficult to imagine yourself being fired at and not feeling afraid. Perhaps that is why I am so glad of this war, because I must know whether or not I am a coward.

I had not long to wait – for the flak, not the answer, I mean.

Essen, in the heart of the Ruhr. On the ground a fire, and round it, on all sides, tracer. Tracer at the rate of 500 rounds a minute, sweeping into the sky to 8,000 feet and then exploding. Zig-zagging, weaving, crossing and re-crossing in all directions: some of it vertical, some diagonal: sometimes straight as an arrow, sometimes straight for a while, then twisting and turning like the Burma road. Red, yellow, green, orange; every colour under the sun, and rising slowly and majestically from the ground. Slowly – how slowly! I could not have thought it possible. Take a tumbler and a bottle of beer. Pour the beer into the glass and then watch the bubbles closely, and you know exactly what tracer looks like: slow at first, then, as it rises, faster. I watched them fascinated, and thought, 'The most powerful firework display in the world, and how pretty! Yes, and that's what they are: a firework display, and put on for my benefit.' But this A.A. was not close. I didn't connect it with danger or with steel and T.N.T., so the picture was not complete. I still needed to know my reactions. It was the same with heavy shells. These, too, I saw at first only in the distance: yellow star-shaped flashes flickering about in the sky. I did not know their lethal range or how far away they were. I idly pictured flying fragments and concussion, but once again they were not close. I did not connect them with danger. It was a stupid feeling, this, flying around watching it, and wondering what it was like to be in the middle of it; and thinking merely: 'How pretty!' Then when I was least expecting it I heard my first shell. At last the real thing: action. People watch action all day: they see it in books and on the screen; on the roads too, every day, but you cannot know action until you're in it, and in this case you're in it only when you hear the shell burst.

I was in the front turret over Duisburg; the target was the docks. We had finished the run-up and the bombs had gone. I was leaning forward over the bomb-sight, craning my neck to try to watch the bursts; they should be bursting any moment now. I was running through my mind what I had done, wondering whether I had forgotten anything, to fuse the bombs or open the doors or switch all the selectors down. The bombs burst, large yellow flashes; not quite on the docks but very close in the area. I was just about to tell Lofty, when Axtell's voice broke. He was so excited I could hardly hear what he was saying; something about a train; something about one minute being there and the next minute not. Lofty told him to pull himself together. A little more calmly, but not much – he seemed to have some restriction lodged in his throat – he said one of the bombs had hit a train and the train had disappeared. Lofty opened his mouth to answer, but it was not he who made the noise, an angry deep-throated roar, like a staccato growl, which jerked the aircraft viciously. Then a rattle as a few pieces of shrapnel came through the fuselage. As Lofty took violent action I had a momentary sinking feeling; my mind flashed on an un-imagined, limitless vista, like the opening of some monstrous floodgate. Somehow it was more than I had bargained for, and not quite so pretty as I used to think. It was personal – very personal. It argued power, cold, unashamed power; the clash of steel and gunpowder against flesh. I sat on my para-chute, thinking somehow it might protect me. Lofty was evading fiercely, twisting and diving and climbing, and the ack-ack was bursting all round, a series of crashes and groans and jerks; sometimes bright flashes and small black mush-room puffs. Then, as suddenly as it had opened, the flood-gate shut. I felt a surge in my heart. The engines sounded defiant, as though they were saying: 'We are the top, this is what we were built for. If there were no opposition we did not have to be so strongly built. This is our life, give us more.' I found I was thinking more clearly. They tell me it is a medical fact that you think clearly when you are afraid. I do not know anything about that. I do not know even that I was afraid, but in this case I found I was thinking more clearly. The visions I had at F.T.S. came back – vividly. They were not so fanciful after all, and I understood suddenly the attraction, the gripping, priceless attraction, of night-bombing. Without ack-ack these flights were just another cross-country; they were dull, something you could find any time, anywhere; but with ack-ack they were changed into something worth having; something that only war could give. And at least I understood this much, that I was not afraid of ack-ack. I am afraid of many things, small, stupid things, things I would not dare talk about, and God knows I have suffered real, hopeless fear, but I am not afraid of ack-ack. It is nothing to be proud of. Fear is only the sum of the play of your imagination, and no two people's imagination plays the same way. A man who walks into a machine-gun without being aware that it is firing at him is not a brave man. No, unfortunately, it is nothing to be proud of, but it is something to cash in on.

On the way home I thought: 'What is ack-ack meant to do? To shoot you down, of course, but I mean what else? After all, the number of shells that they send up is enormous, but the aeroplanes that fall down are very few. I suppose they are meant to put you off reaching the target – well, that's funny, because they don't. Or do they? They don't frighten you away; they naturally make you more determined, but there's something else they do. I can't quite think what it is at the moment, but I soon will. In fact, I think I know already. Yes, of course I do. Yes, it's obvious.' And so it was for the second time that my vision from F.T.S. sank beneath the mire of technical skill. No matter how good a pilot you are, you have got to have this technical skill and this knowledge. You have got to understand the set-up, be able to sit back and know, not have to pause and work it out or rush in wildly, hoping for the best. You have a job to do, to drop some bombs in the right place. That is all. It does not sound much, but it has to come before everything else. The fun and the excitement will come later, when you know how to get results.

In order to get results you have first to reach the target area; in other words, navigate. There is a navigator, of course, whose sole job it is to take you to the target area, but that is not the end of the story. With the aid of some maps and charts and rulers and other varied instruments he is able to tell you your air position – that is to say, where you would be if there were no wind. He can tell you where you actually are only if he knows, and has known ever since take-off, the strength and direction of the wind, or if he has some extraneous means of finding out his position. These means, however, are limited and not entirely reliable. He can discover the wind by taking a series of drift readings on various headings, but this requires good conditions of visibility and exceptionally accurate flying and reading-off from the drift indicator. As for fixing his position, the only infallible method is visual pin-point – by map-reading – and this again, quite naturally, demands good visibility. If he cannot map-read he has to fall back on W/T or Astro, but neither of these is universally accurate, and into the bargain W/T gives the position of the aircraft away, while Astro requires a high degree of training both from the pilot and the navigator. And from all this the residue is D.R. Given the wind velocity, and the aircraft's course and airspeed, the navigator can discover by D.R. his position at any time, but a forecast wind can hardly hope to be accurate enough under war conditions, so he has to be able to check it by some means or other, and in addition the pilot's course must be perfect, or the D.R. position will not be correct. Every deviation from course, every variation in airspeed or alteration in height, adds another mile to the final error. A difference of one degree gives an error of one mile in sixty, and on the compass one degree is almost indistinguishable. On a flight of 600 miles, then, it will be a good crew that has less than a ten-mile error. And so, taken by and large, it is still the captain who looks after 50 per cent of the navigation. The navigator has his instruments and his aids, and these he will, and does, use to the maximum of their limits, but it is for the captain to make them available for him so that he can apply his skill. If there is a full moon and no cloud anywhere the captain has no need to do anything except listen to instructions from the map, but it is only once every few months that such conditions exist. There may be cloud; perhaps at 2,000 feet, perhaps at 15,000; there may be gaps or layers, or bumpy conditions at 6,000 feet, while up at 10,000 feet calm as millwater. Below the clouds it may be the other way round: dark below, and above, perfect for Astro sights. If the captain chooses the wrong height the navigator may have no aids to work on.

Then ack-ack. The gunners, to put a shell near you, need a certain amount of time. First they have to predict your position, your course and your speed, and from that calculate where you will be when the shell bursts. The working out may be done automatically, but none the less it has to be done. Then the shell has to be fused for the right height, the gun aimed, the shell put in the breech, and the gun fired; and after all that the shell has to come up. All this takes time; you have a certain latitude. But once the first shell has arrived, the others will follow fast and furiously; you cannot afford to fly straight and level for long. If you do not fly straight and level you make the navigation less accurate, therefore you want to avoid the defences on the way out. But – there always seems to be a but – if you fly at a reasonable height to give greater immunity the navigator may not be able to map-read, so what are you going to do? It is the same with searchlights; once they hold you, you are blinded completely and all chance of map-reading is gone. At one place it may be safe to come down and see the ground, at another it may be the other way round; better to stay high and use D.R. It is the captain's decision, and if he decides wrong he does not give the navigator much chance.

Once the target is reached, the target itself has to be identified. The problem is the same, except that this time it must be identified by visual pin-point or not at all. If the night is light and the visibility good, there is no problem at all; only the defences. If the night is dark, the only hope is to break the dark with a flare, but that is not so simple an operation. A flare illuminates only a small area, perhaps three or four miles; and not for very long, about three minutes. Someone has to put it in the flare-chute – and it is heavy – set the fuse-setting for the correct height and then launch it. When eventually it lights up it has fallen way back behind the aircraft, so you have to turn about and come back over the top. The flare is powerful; it will dazzle you unless you shield your eyes or look away from it, and if you want to compare what you see on the ground with the map you have to switch a light on or you will not be able to read the map. That takes time and defocuses your eyes. But there is even more to it than that. Map-reading is a navigational aid only when it produces a recognizable pin-point, and recognizable pin-points are not so frequent. Roads or rivers or woods are not pin-points unless they are very distinctive or unless you have been following your track all the way and know what to look for. After 400 or 500 miles without any pin-point you may well be unlucky and not find any recognizable landmark from the light of a dozen flares, even though you are actually within a few miles of the target.

Then the actual dropping of the bombs. Once more the same problem. A bomb, from 10,000 feet, takes about 25 seconds to fall. In that time the aeroplane has moved a mile or so, depending on its speed. To aim the bomb you need a bomb-sight, and a bomb-sight is a complicated instrument, in that it must incorporate the triangle of velocities, the aircraft's height, and the angle of fall of the bomb. These five readings have to be set, and the aircraft steered in such a way that its track, not its course, passes over the target, before there is any hope of success. In short, the run-up must be started at least three miles from the aiming-point, to allow sufficient time for all this, and if it is necessary to use a flare, you will have to drop the flare over the target, fly away far enough, turn round, pick up the target again, adjust the bomb-sight, and make good the right track all before the flare goes out. Crew co-operation must be good or there will not be any results. But every night is different from the last: clouds, visibility, strength of the defences – they all vary. And so it is the captain's decision. Come down or stay up? The lower you are, the faster everything happens, and the better the co-operation has to be. The lower down, too, the more effective the defences; they may blind you altogether, or anyway preclude an accurate run-up. The higher up, the more time to act, and the more immune you are from disturbance, but, on the other hand, the less you can see. It is a vicious circle, and the captain has to unravel it. It is he who plays for position, and when he has finished manoeuvring the stage is set for the navigator to do the best he can. No matter how much you read, or how much you talk to other more experienced captains, you will never learn except by experience, because the same combination of circumstances is not likely to occur twice. The navigator, of course, may know more than the captain, and he is there to give advice, but in the end the decision must be made by one man. There is no time or petrol to talk things over, any more than there is to jump up 10,000 feet and have a look at the weather there, and then drop down again if it does not look so good. If you are to be successful you have to know at a glance how you are going to get the best results. You have to understand that ack-ack can put you off hitting the target and that determination is not the deciding factor and instead you have to know what tactics will, on any given night, beat the combination of weather and ground defence.

As it happened, there was one more vision yet which suffered the same fate – weather. 'Despite severe weather conditions our aircraft pressed home their attack with great determination.' 'Owing to the weather no aircraft of Bomber Command operated last night.' How often have I read those headings in the past six months, and equally how often have I imagined myself battling through storms and snow and ice, and roaring out of sleet and rain on to the target! Again a pretty picture, but that is all. The elements are strong; much too strong. Have you ever stood on the beach at low tide and gazed on rocks, and then thought how easily the sea laps them up when she wishes to? Or watched the anger of her waves? I have, and I am terrified. It is the same with the skies. If you know how, you can beat them; but defy them? That is something you can never do. Low clouds, ten-tenths, all over Germany. Suppose you navigate right to the target area; suppose even you know just where the target is – then what? Come out of the clouds and every searchlight in the place will hold you. Even if they do not you cannot make use of a flare as low as that: the pace is too fast and the illuminated area too small. Anyway, you may fly into the ground. An altimeter works on the density of air, and if the barometric pressure has changed, which it is almost bound to have done, you may be 1,000 feet lower than you think you are. It may be as clear as day in London; people may say:

'Why don't they bomb Berlin?' But if there is continuous cloud over Germany you might as well stay at home and save the petrol. In London city only one yard in every ten is built up; there is not much point in dropping a bomb in Germany at random, just because it is Germany. Bombs cost money. Then again, what are you going to do if you are back over England with low, ten-tenths cloud underneath and hills in the neighbourhood? You can come down if you like, and hope you are where you think you are, but it's hardly worth it.

Even experienced men like Lofty cannot play tricks with the weather. In fact only the other day he went a little too far. Yes, now I come to think of it, it was a good object lesson. I shall remember it, and try to remember, too, that the skies are not quite as pretty and innocuous as they look.

The target had been Cologne, and the weather very bad. As it turned out, we might as well not have gone. Over the North Sea a Cold Front 100 miles wide and reaching to 16,000 feet; another one just north of the target. It was bumpy and wet and altogether unpleasant; we did not find the target, but somewhere we found a reasonable break, with what appeared to be a railway line beneath it. This was better than nothing, so we attacked it, but we could not even tell where the bombs fell. For once it had been an early start; we had crossed the Dutch coast in daylight under the cover of cloud, so we should be back well before dawn. Unfortunately the wireless packed up, and we never saw the stars long enough for Astro, so we had to rely entirely on D.R. and the 'met' winds.

At last E.T.A. English coast. We would be home soon. Thank God. I was fed up with the bumps and the rain pouring in through the windscreen. Lofty flicked his head and took over in his usual manner. A few weeks ago in the half-light I was following the coast up, and, not paying much attention, I failed to notice I had left the sea behind and was over land. It is easy to be confused when the light is bad, but that was no excuse. 'Balloons.' Lofty saw them first, and it was the only time I have ever seen him startled. They were balloons all right. Everywhere: above, below, and on all sides. We were 600 feet: too low to jump and it was hardly worth climbing. There did not seem much point in turning round, either, since we were right in the middle of them, so I carried on straight ahead. Somehow I could not help thinking of Sten and 'Danny Boy'. We sat there still as stone, hoping: well, hardly daring to hope. I can see Lofty's figure now, gaunt and tall and strong, standing beside me in the well, with one foot on the step, vainly trying to pierce the darkness. None of us spoke a word for three minutes till we were safely clear, and then I suspect our voices were slightly nervous. After that Lofty always took over at the coast.

I argued Percy into giving me a map and went to the front turret to look for land. The clouds were worse than ever – base 900 feet and in places down to 400 feet, and, into the bargain, pouring with rain. We were flying at 700 feet – as low as we dared. The weather was expected to be bad at Base, so without wireless our best bet was to break cloud out to sea where there were no hills. As long as we saw and recognized the coast there would be no difficulty.

E.T.A. up five minutes ago; we should be there now. The forward visibility was practically nil, so I kept my eyes glued downwards through the bomb-sight panel. Once or twice I thought I saw land, but it was only an illusion – perhaps a wider stretch of white horses, or a shadow, or something. I picked up the map to see if any part of the coast was higher than we were, because if it was we would never see it in time, and we might easily be off track. But we had to stay below cloud now, so we carried on. The minutes went by – five, ten, twenty. Rain was streaming down the back of my neck, but still no sign of the coast. My eyes were beginning to feel the strain, and I found myself imagining all sorts of weird shapes and forms. Radley was still working away at the set: valves and coils and plugs strewn all over the floor. The half-hour came and went. I asked Percy to take my place for a few moments and let me rest my eyes. Lofty said: 'Go and check the log. Percy has probably added two and three and made sixty-nine.' The log and the chart were incredibly neat. It was an easy job and I checked it very carefully, but there was no mistake there.

'The wind must have changed. We've been flying seven and a half hours, and had no check at all. If it's turned through 180 degrees we can be anything up to 500 miles out. It's very strong.'

'O.K. Well, I think I'll turn west. We must be too far east or we'd have hit the coast long ago. We're probably flying up the North Sea parallel to land.'

'We might have been blown the other way and be heading out to mid-Atlantic.'

'True, O King, but it's not likely.'

'We've got to make up our minds one way or the other.'

'Let's have another shot at taking a drift; that will give us an idea.'

We dropped a flame float and tried, but the visibility was too poor. Lofty turned west.

'What course are you steering?'

'Two hundred and eighty.'

Percy laid it off on the chart and I went back to the front turret. Once more the minutes ticked by. Now and then patches of higher cloud, but very few. Axtell suddenly burst into conversation for the first time since take-off:

'We've just crossed the coast.'

The blasé way he said it made me laugh.

'Doesn't look like it to me.'

'I know it's land because I've just seen a wood.'

'O.K., we'll drop a flare.'

At great trouble to everyone, except Axtell, we pulled a flare out of its stowage, fused it, dropped it, and circled round; but below there was nothing but sea. A heap of abuse fell upon Axtell's head, but all he said was: 'Must have fallen asleep and dreamt it.'

My imagination began to play tricks. First we were out in the Atlantic; then we were right over to the east near the Danish coast. In either of these cases it would be best to turn round and make for land, because if we came down in the sea without wireless no one would know where we were. Stupid, because, looking at the thing logically, we could not be far away; but that was what I said an hour ago, and, anyway, the dark and the rain and the efforts of searching seem to make you think these strange thoughts.

Lofty grew tired: told me to come and take over. Having to concentrate on flying was a pleasant change. I looked at the instruments and thought: 'Just a few luminous figures and some pointers, and sea below, and eight and a quarter hours since we took off, and not very much petrol, and a long time ago bombs somewhere on Germany, and we don't know where we are, and these few pointers and figures are going to bring us home. What a curious life!' Axtell said: 'May I leave my turret for a moment, Captain?' I looked at my watch: 4.25. 'One hundred minutes overdue, and in twelve hours' time I shall be having tea with Lorna – I hope.' The port engine spluttered and I changed over on to the last tank. One hour to go. Well, an hour is quite a long time. Percy gave me some coffee. Good old Percy; he had a smudge of chocolate on his left cheek. It was a little lighter; not very much, but still just a little. The rain had not stopped; I thought it seemed worse than ever, and water was pouring in through the joints in the perspex, dripping on to my right knee and left hand. Drip, drip. Nothing but drip all the time. It was irritating – foully irritating. The cloud base was still the same, 900 feet, with occasional murky wisps reaching down lower. I wriggled in my seat and thought: 'Glad it's Lofty's responsibility and not mine.' Lofty had not spoken for fifteen minutes.

Vaguely, out of the corner of my eye, I saw a faint darkish line flash below us. 'Land!' Before I could say anything Lofty shouted: 'Turn through 90 degrees. Hurry, man, for God's sake! We're right on top of it, and it's high ground.' I pulled everything for all I was worth and we shot round, and Percy slid off his seat, cursing. 'Follow the coast down south till I find out where we are.' When we were heading more or less in the right direction I took my eyes off the compass and kept them on the coast. Great commotion and confabulation from Lofty and Percy. Maps and torches flying all over the place. Somehow the coast seemed to be a very curious shape. I felt it was going round in circles. Also what I could see of it appeared very unfamiliar. Lofty said: 'Keep on flying south;

44

I can't pick anything out yet.' I looked over to port, and my heart leapt. The coast was over there now; the sea was on the wrong side, too. Help, I must have fallen to sleep! I looked back; no, the coast is on the starboard too. It's on both sides.

'What the b— hell are you playing at?'

'Following the coast, as you said.'

'Come on, pull your finger out, man, you're over land, and these things are hills, not clouds.'

Yes, they were too.

'What course are you steering?'

'I don't know; the compass is still turning, and I haven't set the gyro for some time. Hang on a moment, it's settling down. God in heaven!'

'What's the matter?'

'We're flying north.'

'Well, don't blame me. Turn on to 180 and for pity's sake keep out to sea.'

I turned round and kept on flying. The coast was the most extraordinary shape I have ever seen: islands and inlets and hills, and all the time rain. For all I knew it might be Ireland or Norway or Scotland. Then suddenly Lofty came out of the well and twisted my nose for all he was worth, till I had to kick him away. He said:

'It's O.K., we're miles north. Do you want a spell, Cheddar?'

'No, thanks.'

Flashes on the ground to starboard.

'What was that?'

'Hell, they're firing at us!'

'Ack-ack behind, Captain.'

'Shut up, Axtell, for God's sake. Give them the recognition signal.'

'What is it?'

'I don't know: Percy's lost the log.'

'It must be on the floor under those maps.'

'Ack-ack still following us, Captain; you'd better get weaving.'

'Axtell, I'll break your ruddy neck.'

I headed out to sea and we landed safely, and I kept my

date with Lorna, and, if it comes to that, our next four trips were very successful, but none the less I think I will get to know more about this weather of ours. I think I'll ask Lofty: he seemed to know by instinct which way to turn. But Lofty's voice woke me up:

'Come and take over, Cheddar.'

'O.K., Cap.'

'That's the last time you'll ever hear me say that.'

'Christ – what's happened?'

'Tomorrow you're going to be a captain.'

CHAPTER THREE

CAPTAINCY

Very early August and a beautiful evening. Desmond and I
arm in arm walking back to camp. Two sprogs: the two most
junior pilot officers of the Squadron, but none the less a
partnership. For good or evil, through thick and through
thin, a partnership – second pilot and captain. At least, that
was the way we drank our toasts. 'The world may come and
the world may go, but no one thinks we're any good, so to
hell with them.'

Outside the mess a group of men were standing; an aircraft was approaching from the south.

'What do you think that is?'

'A Whitley three.'

'No, it's not; too small.'

'Hampden.'

'Don't be b— silly – sounds like a Wellington'; and so
forth. As it came overhead I saw its silhouette plainly – a
Junkers 88.

Desmond and I ran headlong into the open, the others into
the mess, and the bombs fell 150 yards away in the middle of
the camp, but miraculously missed all buildings.

And so, having work to do in the morning, we went to
bed.

The morning was busy – air test and talking things over
with the crew – Desmond, second pilot; Stokey, wireless
operator; Howard, navigator; Pike, rear gunner, and aircraft 'N' for Nuts. I could not really ask for anything better.
All of them were good and Stokey was the best operator in
the Squadron. Eight-fifty-two in the evening the wheels left
the ground. The target was Cologne marshalling yard; the
weather bad, but that did not damp my excitement. A stream
of white vapour sprayed out of the port engine as we crossed

the aerodrome boundary and I felt an awful sickening feeling lest we should have to turn back. It went on for some time, then suddenly stopped: glycol from the overflow vent; I should have known better. Past the coast I handed over to Desmond. I had no idea how he flew, so best to find out straightaway. While he settled down and fixed himself to his liking, which turned out to be a lengthy proceeding, we were flown about in every conceivable direction, but after that he was good, very good. The weather was certainly bad. Cloud base 2,000 feet and stretching up to 6,000 or 7,000. We needed a drift to check up our track over the sea, so in spite of the bumps we stayed below cloud. I dropped a flame float, and while Pike stood by to take a reading from the rear turret I watched over Desmond's shoulder to see if his course was steady.

'O.K., Pike?'

'Six degrees port.'

'We'll take another one to check it.'

Same procedure again.

'What's it this time?'

'Four degrees starboard.'

'That's not much help. We'll have to skip it and blame the bumps. Better climb up above these clouds. I'm going into the front turret.'

I tested the guns and all the auxiliary equipment, in particular setting the 'met' wind on the bomb-sight, and settled down to meditate. It was very bumpy and as much rain seemed to be coming in the turret as in the pilot's seat. After twenty minutes I looked at the altimeter – 2,500 feet: it must have gone U.S. I went back to the cabin and looked at the instrument panel – 2,500 feet also.

'I told you to climb.'

'I can't.'

'What's the matter?'

'Nothing that I can see, I just can't get her to climb.'

'Engines O.K.?'

'Yes, I can get full revs and boost all right.'

'Controls?'

'Bit sloppy, that's all.'

'Temperature, pressures all O.K. Low-speed super-charger: weak mixture; no icing. It beats me altogether. If the engines are giving the right power she must climb. What about the trim? Are you sure one engine hasn't stopped? It won't show on the gauges unless the motor seizes, you know.'

'No, I thought of that.'

'Well, we'll just have to carry on at this height and hope for the best, that's all.'

I checked the navigation. There was not much to do: to date we had nothing to go on, only D.R. Came back beside Desmond and watched over his flying. E.T.A. coast 35 minutes. Somehow it struck me that something was wrong. Yet everything seemed all right. I checked it carefully; then once again. Definitely all correct, yet I could not get rid of the feeling. I was staring straight ahead at the starboard panel and thought:

'What a pretty colour that green light is, but it should be dimmed a bit – too bright: reflects on the perspex.'

I was chewing gum and the peppermint flavour had gone, damn it. Then suddenly it dawned on me. The light was green, it ought to be red.

'Desmond, you b— fool, your undercarriage is down!'

He pulled the lever up and started muttering to himself. It was as much my fault as his, but it made me laugh.

'Shall I carry on climbing?'

'Yes, get above this muck for God's sake: 8,000 feet.'

Just before E.T.A. the Dutch coast I took over. The clouds were below us now, 10/10ths, and therefore no sign of land, not even of searchlights or guns.

'We'll have to get radio help until this weather lifts.'

I concentrated on flying a straight and level course and Stokey got some bearings, dozens of them. The clouds began to thin out and a few searchlights appeared – pools of light wafting across below us – at least we were over enemy territory. Howard worked the bearings out and shook his head.

'We'll have to carry on on D.R. then. The weather looks like it's improving, so we should be able to pick up the Rhine. Pity, though, the moon's obscured.'

'Searchlights getting busy.'

'Yes, at least it must be a defended area. Anyway, we've plenty of time to hang around and look.'

A few orange flashes appeared, rolling zig-zag across the clouds beneath us – ack-ack. Very scattered, but a few seemed to be predicted on us. I began to take evasive action; my first effort really and I found it rather a strain. Twisting and turning was easy enough, but it was concentrating on averaging the turns out into the right course that was difficult. I found myself tending to keep turning away from the bursts rather than equal out by using the same number of degrees each side. There was no serious opposition at all, so I was able to practise, and that was just as well. Howard went into the front turret and map-read, but with no success. The clouds had practically gone, perhaps 3/10ths at 5,000 feet, but it was pitch dark and, I thought, hazy on the ground. Every now and then I looked round at Desmond to see what his reactions were. An intense look of interest on his face, determined not to miss anything, and regarding the whole thing as a gigantic side-show put on for his benefit. It made me laugh and reminded me of my first trip. Well, it certainly was a sight for the gods: even the searchlights by themselves – feathery, rock-blue shafts, like giant fingers probing and prying about in the heavens. I think perhaps it is the subconscious background, the human inability to understand the depths and the heights of a twentieth-century war, that fosters such excitement in these ordinary, mechanical phenomena.

E.T.A.

'May as well drop a flare for luck.'

'Flare gone.'

I waited a few moments, keeping on the same course, then an orange glow appeared behind the wing. I turned sharply through 180° and circled round, keeping the port wing between the flare and myself so as not to be blinded. Details were not clear at all – it must definitely have been hazy: trees, woods, fields vaguely and, I thought, hills, but nothing else; nothing to show whereabouts we were.

'This isn't much good; we might drop flares all night at

this rate and still not get a pin-point. What is the general trend of the bearings, east or west?'

'East.'

'O.K.; we'll fly west and try to pick up the Rhine. We should be able to see it in spite of the visibility.' We *should* have been able to, but we did not. Up and down, back and forth, for an hour and forty minutes, but no Rhine. Instead, bunches of searchlights and a few shells. Another Whitley flashed by a few feet overhead, going in the opposite direction. Clouds here and there and everywhere pitch dark. Once we saw a stick of bombs explode and some incendiaries burning – white and blue pin-points dancing about beneath us. We flew over to them and dropped a flare, but nothing to recognize: a factory, perhaps: I was not sure. Other people's flares too, but all over the place and therefore no help. Some A.A. opened up suddenly, quite close, to port and underneath. A few thumps and rattles and then it stopped. Desmond seemed to enjoy it. One by one the flares disappeared, and not once did we get a pin-point. I tried flying into concentrations of searchlights and A.A. to see what they were defending, but without success. Either they were much further off than I thought or else they seemed to melt away as we came near. Stokey became very disgruntled in the fuselage. It was dark there, for without blacking out the windows he could not switch the light on, and very uncomfortable too. I was taking avoiding action most of the time; he had nowhere to hold on to – only the floor to sit on, and he could not tell what was going on. I became restless too, for the task seemed hopeless. I didn't know where we were and now only one flare left. We had to bomb on this one or not at all. I waited another ten minutes, picked out the largest concentration of searchlights and flew into it. For the last time Stokey dropped a flare. For the last time too I saw the orange glow behind the wing and circled round. I caught my breath.

'I think – I think— Yes, by God, it is! Not Cologne, but anyway quite a fair-sized town. There's a railway station in it too. Can you see it, Howard? O.K. I'm losing height. Have to be a short run-up, the flare won't last much longer. Think

I'm heading towards it; you'll have to take over now.' Desmond went down the well to look for results through the drift-sight hatch, and Howard started giving directions. Bomb-doors open and bombs fused. Stokey came forward from the flare-chute. 'Left, left.' Then Pike's voice broke in:

'Searchlights have got us.'

They had, too, and on all sides.

'Have to ignore them till the bombs have gone – not much longer.'

'Hard to port. O.K. Steady. Damn these searchlights!'

'Keep your head right down, don't look ahead or they'll blind you.'

'What height?'

'1,900 – air speed 130. I'm gliding.'

'Right a bit. Steady.'

'Ack-ack, sir. Tracer, falling behind.'

'O.K. Keep off the wire unless it's very close.'

'Steady, steady.'

289 on the gyro. I kept my eye glued on it.

'Bombs gone.'

'Ack-ack closer, sir.'

'Look for the bomb-bursts: whatever you do, try to see the bomb-bursts.'

I opened up, full revs and boost, and started to take evasive action. Took my eye off the instruments and looked around, but soon gave that up. The searchlights were on all sides, in a circle, dozens of them. They blinded me completely. The aircraft was shining bright, like luminous paint, inside as well as out. Desmond came back and flopped beside me. Normally I am scared to do anything except the very gentlest turns at night, but now it came naturally, as though I had done it all my life. We dived and we banked and we stall-turned – everything under the sun – and most of the time I did not know what attitude we were in. As often as not I seemed to be looking up at the ground and not down. Now and then we broke clear of the lights, but they soon clamped down again. There is an air of finality about searchlights. Wherever you turn or look they are still there, staring at you. Nothing seems to happen much – at least, not in this instance: such guns as there were were not very accurate. It is the feeling of being trapped, like a nightmare, running away from some shape, and every time you escape him he looms up bigger than ever just in front of you. That gets on my nerves. Pike was having the time of his life, firing away for all he was worth. How his guns didn't melt, God knows. He said he had put some of the lights out, but it didn't seem to make much difference. Suddenly, as I was looking at the gyro – we were heading almost due south – I realized what a damn' fool I was. I turned on to 090 and kept the general direction until we were out of range of the lights. It occurred to me I had been flying round in a circle for the last seven minutes inside the cone, giving them all the practice they wanted instead of breaking straight out and putting up with the illumination until we were too far for them to hold us any longer. Well, anyway, it was a good lesson. I only hope the rest of the crew did not realize it too. I climbed on course to 6,000 feet and saw the Dutch coast through a gap; 40 miles to starboard of track. I had no map, but Howard was sure of the pin-point.

'Some of these fixes were right after all, then. We must have come down on E.T.A. miles east of the target.'

The winds had previously veered right round and we had not been able to check them. Pity. Looking at a map in the front turret, I had a nasty shock.

'Good God, if we were east of Cologne we must have been in the hills. Some of them are over 2,000 feet and we were down to 1,500.'

No wonder the searchlights looked as if they were shining down on us. I turned in my seat and drank some coffee. Hills always have frightened me, even when I was a small boy. I looked back to see how the others felt, but it didn't seem to worry them in the least. Stokey was working away like a one-armed paperhanger with the itch, Howard was asleep, and Desmond scowling over the controls. I thought: 'I'm supposed to be in charge of these marvellous people, but I haven't done my job very well. Lofty would have done a lot better.' And so I wrote the trip off as experience and thereby gained solace.

A night off, and then some glorious news. Italy. I had missed the last trip and it had nearly broken my heart, but maybe it was just as well. The weather had been terrible – electrical storms and fronts and icing and God knows what. Only two crews had crossed the Italian frontier. This time the weather promised to be very good. Feverish activity and an early start: we were working from Advanced Base. I collected the crew together and all our gear too. That was the greatest problem. We had not put it away after Cologne and now some of it was missing. Oxygen. I had forgotten all about that: never used it before and so I had neglected to have my mask fitted. An added complication too, 'N' had gone U.S. – glycol leak. We would have to take Queenie instead. That infuriated Stokey; he carried his own receiver around with him and refused to use any other, which meant he would have to take it out of Nuts and put it into 'Q'. At the last moment I remembered we had forgotten the thermos flasks, and Desmond had to dash off to the mess to collect them; but in the end we got off, a quarter of an hour after the others. Desmond took over the navigation on the way down. Stokey had to put his Oppenheimer away and get a bearing, and Flight Commander Maxy cursed us for arriving an hour late.

Advanced Base had never known such an influx before, but they were good friends. A first-class tea – ham and eggs – and I dispatched Desmond to supervise refuelling. We could use every drop the tank would hold and I wanted to make certain. Myself and Howard found a quiet corner for flight-planning. Route – Eastbourne and direct to target. We could find no advantage in any other route. The latest 'met' forecast came in as we were working: even better than the earlier one had suggested. Navigation should be easy. I made a mental note that lakes in mountains have their pitfalls: unless you are right overhead they look a different shape. Then rang up sergeants' mess to check on state of guns and wireless and joined Desmond for a drink in our mess.

Zero hour as you might expect: 27 Whitleys massed for a non-stop take-off. An impressive sight watching them nose cautiously out on to the tarmac, to the roar of 648 Rolls-

Royce cylinders. 26 took off. Jimmy stayed on the ground. Poor old Jimmy, if ever anyone deserved to go it was he. First reserve for the last trip, and he missed that too. I had been through it with Jimmy from the start – 15 stone of pure muscle and, as is so often the case, a heart of gold. I would rather see anyone stay behind than Jimmy. I thought of the Milanese – poor saps: little did they know – and by mistake set course in the opposite direction, due north.

A perfect evening, we could ask for nothing better. On the starboard a rosy hue was ushering the sun out of sight. On the port, dusk creeping slowly closer. Below, the sea was as calm as oil, not a sign of white horses anywhere. Desmond was flying and I wanted to sit back and enjoy the colours, but it was not as simple as that. It was still daylight and German fighters must be on patrol. The clouds were not much help either – 3/10ths at about 2,000 feet. The lower down, of course, the darker it would be – there is probably enough light to see an aircraft at 15,000 feet 45 minutes after the end of twilight on the ground – but I did not want to cross the French coast right down on the deck. Told everybody to keep a strict look-out, especially on the dark side: that's where they would come from. As the time rolled by and the dark came closer and closer we started to climb.

'E.T.A. coast up 17 minutes.'

'O.K. Get up to 7,000 feet and hold it.'

Clouds were closing in: it did not look as though we would see the coast at all. We didn't either, nor any fighters.

Well inland, past Paris, the clouds began to break. Desmond had been flying for over two hours: he was getting restless. I checked up on the navigation and took over. For some curious reason W/T reception was very bad. Stokey managed to pass up a phenomenal number of bearings. Howard sorted them out and plotted two fixes: showed us 2° to starboard of track.

'Shall I alter course on them?'

'No, I don't think so. But work out our track made good on the assumption they are O.K., and if we don't see anything on E.T.A. we'll set course from where the fixes put us.'

Below, many twinkling lights – blackout very bad but not

much help; too many towns and villages for pin-points. Clouds almost completely gone. Began to climb to clear the Alps; a long, wearisome business, but we got there in the end. The lights and the sparkling stars set my mind wondering. At the back, my eyes were fixed on the instruments, and subconsciously my limbs kept adjusting the compass-needle to where it belonged, but my thoughts were far, far away.

Last night – one of the most surprising nights I have ever spent. Jimmy and I hitched ourselves a lift up to town, 26 miles up the coast. The sun was hot and the sands sparkling. and the sea looked warm even if it was not, so we bathed. There was no sweet young girl to rub the sand out of my feet, but none the less it was a wonderful afternoon. Tea was wonderful too, and having digested it we set out to discover what the town had to offer. For the first hour and a half not much to report: a round of the bars and Jimmy talking at the top of his voice about women's hair styles, but no promise of any developments. At the fourth port of call the outlook was better – tinkling glasses and jewellery and laughter. Jimmy's eyes brightened and his step became jaunty. Needless to say he settled himself down beside the most gorgeous girl in the room and from then on appeared to have forgotten my presence completely. Occasionally I caught sight of a pair of deep-blue eyes misted over with a sort of happy wistful expression, but that was all. Occasionally, too, I heard a quiet, tender voice saying, 'Same again?', but he did not appear to be talking to me.

Some time later, much later, I found a most extraordinary place: smoke-bound atmosphere and remarkable-tasting whisky and people playing chemmy. Jimmy had disappeared to find his girl and I had no money to gamble, but it was an amusing three-quarters of an hour. At midnight the gaming began to grow animated, and I left. Outside there was a wonderful smell of salt, so I set out for the beach. The district was unfamiliar: rows and rows of dirty-looking houses and no one to ask the way. I must have walked in many circles. At last I saw the sea, but between it and me barbed-wire entanglements, so it was some time before I managed to break through. When I eventually reached the shore it was well worth the effort and a torn tunic. Sea and moon and the quiet splash of breakers. I wandered slowly up and down with my hands in my pockets, thinking I had the laugh on Jimmy after all, but unfortunately not for very long. Dimly I heard a heavy step behind me, and then:

'Halt. Who goes there?'

'Friend.'

'Advance and be recognized.'

I advanced cautiously: the bayonet looked menacing.

'What's the password?'

'Don't know.'

'Have you your permit?'

'No; I've my R.A.F. pass, though.'

'Does it permit you on a defended area?'

'I don't think so. I didn't know this was a defended area.'

'In that case you'll have to accompany me to Headquarters.' And so we marched along, I in front with my hands in the air and he behind with a bayonet sticking into my back!

'I hope that gun's not loaded.'

'Well, you hope wrong.'

'At least it's not cocked.'

'Yes, it is. And the safety-catch is off, and I've got my finger on the trigger, but you needn't worry, I haven't taken up the slack on the first pull yet.'

'Well, that's nice to know, anyway.'

I think he was an Australian. The officer in charge was no less menacing, but in the end he broke down. I was given a drink of rum and politely ushered out of the defences. The time was 2.30 Sunday morning, and no trains till half past ten: in fact the station was locked up. No buses either and no Jimmy, and nine o'clock duty at camp. I tried sleeping on the grass outside the Pavilion, but it was too cold. I climbed the station gates and went to sleep in a first-class railway coach, wondering where it was bound for if it should happen to move off.

Half past four found me walking the southbound highway to camp. Town was some five miles behind. I had been lucky and got two lifts so far, but there was still a long way to go. The morning was gorgeous, just as the night had been. I did not mind walking in the least: in fact, come to that, I did not mind whether I arrived back in time or not. If you are in the process of enjoying something, there is no point in spoiling it by worrying. At least that is how I figure it out. Five-thirty found me still walking. Felix the cat had done the same thing once upon a time, but none the less it was quite amusing. In the distance there was something parked by the roadside. I began speculating on what it was. As I came closer I saw it was a car, and a pretty smart-looking car at that. Imperceptibly my pace quickened. A chance of a lift, and I was afraid lest it should move off before I reached it. At least there was somebody in it because they were blowing the horn as though they were in a London jam. Only a hundred yards to go and I was walking fast. Then suddenly I came to a dead stop. I do not think I have ever seen such a beautiful girl, and it wasn't because I was not prepared for it. What was more, she drove me all the way to camp in a beautiful Delage. She had flaming red hair, and when I asked her to have dinner with me she did not refuse. Quite like a story-book. Up here amongst the moon and these fleecy clouds I can hardly believe it happened. I must cross-examine Jimmy closely in the morning. Someone was saying something. My mind rolled over once and I woke up.

'Yes, captain speaking.'

'Are you levelling out now?'

'Yes, 16,500. Gives us about 1,000 feet to spare.'

'O.K., Cap.'

The moon was high in the sky: almost at the peak of her orbit and almost full. Ahead, the foothills of the Alps began to appear. In the aircraft, a quiet air of excitement: I could feel it in my bones; Stokey even put his book down every now and then and gazed out of the window. I plugged in the oxygen and spoke awhile to the rear gunner. We were over the frontier now: over Switzerland. What a marvellous sight! Lights. Everywhere lights: hundreds of them, small clusters, large clusters, lanes of lights and single lights: all burning away cheerfully. Desmond began gesticulating: talking at the same time. Howard was talking too. Ahead in the sky there were a series of huge flashes.

'I wonder if that's the target: someone must have been flying mighty fast, though. Perhaps the Swiss are firing – they are entitled to – but what enormous flashes! I can't judge the range – looks just in front. No, it's all around. It beats me altogether: there aren't any flashes on the ground, so it can't very well be guns.'

For twenty-five minutes we looked down on this mighty panorama of mountains and lakes and snow and ice and illuminated life. Not always down either: on each side of us the peaks rose almost to our own level: sometimes even above us. Travellers have paid hundreds of dollars to see this very same sight, but I doubt if it can ever have meant more to them than it did to us. Patches of cumulonimbus appeared; huge greyish folds towering into the skies; beautiful but dangerous. We skirted round them. Howard found a pinpoint – 23 miles to starboard of track. The fixes were right after all then: good for Stokey. We altered course for the target, and as the Alps fell away beneath us we started losing height. Visibility was much poorer now than it had been: the patches of cumulus were thicker and in addition definite ground haze. On E.T.A. we were down to 4,000 feet. No sign of gunfire, but a few flares about, most of them way up above us. The ground was still indistinct, so we dropped another 1,000 feet. Number 2 tank almost empty: I changed over on to Number 1 so as to avoid any possibility of the engines cutting at a critical moment. The lack of gunfire was suspicious: it might be that the crews were asleep, but then again it might be a trap. I kept a wary eye for any sign of opposition and let Howard do most of the searching. Just as well to be cautious until we knew more about the Italians. We were looking for a landmark north of the town. It could not be far away. Stokey dropped a flare, but because of the haze it was no help. What the object of dropping them 10,000 feet above us was God knows.

Then came the ack-ack and I knew there was no trap.

Howard found the landmark; at least, we all found it at the same time. Great excitement as Howard gave us the course and E.T.A. to the target – 157°: 4½ minutes. Bomb-doors open, bombs fused and Stokey came out of the fuselage: but nothing happened. The town showed up, but no details: perhaps there was smoke from the chimneys. Back to the landmark and the same procedure all over again – twice. The second time we dropped a flare, but apart from a black mass of something we could not identify it as the target. The third time someone dropped a flare on us and hit us squarely in the middle: made an awesome noise, but otherwise no damage. Away to starboard two beautiful fires were burning.

'This is our last chance, Howard; we're already six minutes overdue and we've got to climb up again to clear the Alps. Check that course over: we must be able to find the damned place.

'I have checked it – three times: 197 – 4½ minutes.'

'Nine?'

'Yes, nine.'

'Seven, eight, nine?'

'Yes, that's what I said.'

'You b— fool, I thought you said five. Well, anyway, we've got it this time.'

I turned on and set course.

'Coming down a bit lower. Look out for the railway, you must be able to see it from this height.'

Desmond said: 'Put your navigation lights on.'

I did, but either the gunners couldn't see it or else their shooting was as bad as it looked.

'We're heading straight for that fire. I wonder if it can be the target. My God, it is! The northern end of the factory is completely gutted. I can see flames coming out of the windows. Boy, what a sight!'

'I'll bomb the southern sheds. Piece of cake. Bomb-doors open.'

'They are open. Turning on now, heading about 260. One stick – no time for two.'

Yes, it was a piece of cake too. We all saw the southern shed blow up, and we were not the only ones who had been successful. Into the bargain someone had started a fire on the seaplane base. There should be some good lines at interrogation. The moon, now that everything was over, was descending from her throne; the twinkling lights of Switzerland too were gone, as if bored. The world was asleep: Desmond probably as well: the Milanese possibly not. We were behindhand. A pity, it would be daylight before we crossed the French coast. I told the crew to relax for an hour so that they would be on the top line when the time came, but when the time did come nothing happened. We crossed the coast at 50 feet and in broad daylight, but nothing attacked us. Thirty-five minutes later we reached Eastbourne and, as we had done nine hours previously, identified ourselves, just in case.

We were delayed at Advanced Base owing to slight engine trouble, and arrived back the next day at lunchtime in a very bad temper.

'Desmond, I've cut a date.'

'Who with?'

'Scarlet.'

'Well, ring her up.'

'I don't know her name: forgot to ask her.'

'Well, that's up to you.'

'Oh, I'll find her all right, I know the number of her car.'

'What the hell's that?'

Air-raid siren. Nobody moved, but I got up and walked towards the door: someone said, 'Cissy', and I said, 'So what?' – just as we all say when we cannot think of a suitable come-back. Actually I only started to say it, because before I had finished there was the whine of a bomb, and in spite of my lead, I was not first to the door. I picked up my cap and gas mask. There was more noise than I had ever heard before and I was not frightened; just dazed, too dazed. I reached the door; there were three men there like statues. One of them said:

'Bombs; can't go yet.'

I looked up and saw a bunch of them coming out of the sky. I didn't know anything could move so fast. Out of the corner of my eye I saw some aircraft diving. I said, 'God!' and ran. Well, I didn't run: I got, because I had to. It was only fifteen yards, but that was fifteen yards too far. I finished up head first down the concrete well of the shelter, and the only damage done was caused by the window-frame and bricks that caught me up. I scrambled to my feet, for Desmond was looming up fast – very fast. I couldn't get out of the way in time and caught the full weight of his twelve stone. Good old Desmond, he only just made it. We looked into each other's eyes and laughed. Thank God we did.

We stayed there for twenty minutes – long minutes too. The Wing Commander was beside us in the entrance: white, but very calm, helping to pass the injured inside. Melvin produced a pack of cards and said, 'Anyone like a game of bridge?' But that didn't fool anybody. Tony was there too, dressed in a blanket and trembling: he had been asleep in his bed when the wall came in to wake him. The noise never stopped for an instant. Bombs all the time: nothing but bombs, and somewhere machine-gun fire. Once the shelter shook until I thought it must collapse, and once we went out to bring in Salty. I did not know it was Salty at the time: there was too much blood and cordite; in fact everybody seemed to be blood and cordite. The atmosphere got thick and the Wing Commander asked us not to smoke unless our nerves needed soothing. There were no cigarettes after that, but not because our nerves were calm. The Major produced a tomato and ate it; it struck me as a funny colour against his blackened face and clothes. He was the only man among us at ease, and I looked at his long rows of medals with more respect than ever. Just outside the shelter a wooden hut had caught fire. There were 500,000 rounds of ammunition and they were exploding like peas being shelled. Had been for five minutes. There was a curious thick smell too – we thought it was gas. I tried to act as though I didn't care, but gave it up – it didn't work. A stretcher-party doubled past. From outside, confused shouting and a sound like stampeding horses. Ginger, John, and a W.A.A.F. hurled themselves into the shelter, only just in time as far as I could make out, but it was difficult to grasp the sequence of events. The Wing Commander looked at his watch and asked how Salty was. Someone said something: I can't quite remember what. There was a final soul-breaking crash: a sound of distant machine-gun fire, and the 'All Clear' rang out.

Desmond and I walked up to the hangars. The damage was not as great as it might have been, but there were a lot of bricks and holes I had not seen before. Queenie was in the hangar smoking away her last gasp: she had been hit by an incendiary. Blondie of the ground crew was standing beside her, watching. He said:

'She died where she was born – in the hangar. I knew they would not get her.'

I asked him if there were any casualties among the men and went along to roll-call: two killed and four injured. There had been a direct hit on a shelter. A W.A.A.F. had been killed, also a horse and a civilian. I don't think they ever found the civilian: he was sitting on a wall and got a direct hit. I hung around for a while to see if there was anything to be done, then wandered back to salvage my belongings. The mess had certainly earned its name today, and I could not find my room. I lay down on the grass and tried to collect my thoughts. The local army rang up to ask if a party of men could come over for a bath and the Station Commander said he was sorry, but we were busy.

At six o'clock I walked into the local cinema with Verran. The villagers all stood and stared at us. Our tunics were still stained and torn, but it was not that. Their expression said: 'Good lord, there's still someone left alive!' All the time during the film I kept thinking: 'What a funny war this is! One minute you're in the middle of guns and blood, and the next you're watching Bing Crosby playing the fool.' But, as they say, I will have to get used to it. I guess I'm too impressionable.

For the next ten days the Germans came hard and often; by night and by day, but mostly by night. Of the 26 aircraft that dived out of the sky that fateful lunchtime, not one reached its base. From the attackers' point of view it was a fine achievement. I take my hat off to the men who took part, but it was too costly to be repeated, and the night raids that followed were for the most part not so successful. None the less the moral effect was noticeable. From now on a siren galvanized us into action, and on more nights than one I slid out of bed and wandered about in the open until the bombs had fallen. The first night was the worst of all. My nerves were still frayed from ten hours previously, and the moan of the siren set my stomach tingling and parched my mouth until I felt like gasping for breath. However, as the days went by, our reactions returned gradually to normal. One morning my batman woke me and said:

'Terrible do you had last night, sir.'

'What on earth are you talking about?'

He looked at me somewhat inquiringly.

'Those bombs that fell by the mess.'

I knew there had been no bombs, because I had not left camp all night, so I lost my temper and told him in future not to listen to rumours. Curiously enough, every word of what he had said turned out to be perfectly correct. I must be a sound sleeper.

The Germans were not the only ones who provided diversion during those ten days. I called on the local police and asked for the red-haired owner of a Delage car, number BFX 102. They were very nice, but told me to go to hell. This gave cause for violent thought, but after delving into every conceivable possibility it was obvious there was nothing else for it. I went to town and made a statement charging the driver of the Delage, number BFX102, with dangerous driving in the early hours of last Friday morning. In point of fact it was not very far off the truth. The effect was dynamic. We met in a small room in the police station and I found out quite a number of interesting details. Her name, Maxine, and of no fixed abode. After a pleasant exchange of formalities, which left the sergeant visibly shaken, my statement was read out. It was a good story, simple but effective, about walking peacefully along a deserted country road, a sudden death-defying roar, and a sudden but timely leap to safety among the nettles. It was effective because the outcome was simple. A quiet, friendly argument to start with: a tender apology from Maxine, accompanied by an explanation of the vigorous refreshment inspired by early dawn: a pleased acknowledgment by the sergeant of the broadmindedness and understanding of youth, interspersed, of course, by a few disparaging remarks on the dangers of fast driving: and finally my withdrawing of the charge. Yes, the plan was brilliantly conceived and brilliantly executed; but there was one factor I had overlooked. The sergeant had no sooner smacked his lips on the final word of my statement than Maxine said:

'How did you manage to get my number?'

'As you were disappearing into the distance, of course. I've got good eyesight.'

'Well, that's remarkable; I haven't had a rear plate for three weeks.'

If the sergeant was shaken before, he was electrocuted now. The bored look had gone, and in its place was, I thought, a slight air of triumph. As he worked hard over his pencil he was breathing deeply, and then every now and then grunting. Maxine smiled demurely and said something about meaning to report it for some time but not quite having the courage to face the police. The sergeant looked pleased and said:

'We're not so terrible: not if you don't do anything you shouldn't.'

Then after hours of writing and taking of evidence and signing he went out to look at the car. Of course there was no number-plate. I could have sworn there had been one last Friday, but it was too late now; I had given myself away long ago. The sergeant leaned across to Maxine and spoke in a very confidential voice:

'Has this young man been molesting you?'

'No more than the others really. I think I've seen him around once or twice, but I haven't taken much notice of him.' This seemed to be just what the sergeant wanted. He grunted awhile to himself, stroked his jaw, and after a suitable pause threatened me with various charges such as obstructing the police in the course of their duty and malicious prosecution, until finally I escaped.

Maxine said: 'Of course you want a lift, don't you?'

'Yes, please.'

'Well, it's going to be fun watching you talk your way out of this frame-up, so I don't mind helping you just this once.'

* * *

Stuttgart. A long way and a new navigator. Taffy was his name, and a Welshman. Wavy fair hair, a sparkle in his eye and a scar below his chin. I liked Taffy as soon as I saw him.

'I've been put down on your crew, sir.'

'Good show,' and he said 'Thanks', as though he meant it. That was nice.

Well, of the trip, not much to report. I had to work harder than usual. With Howard we had more or less settled down: he knew his part in the act and I trusted him. With Taffy it could not be so as yet. I had to pester him to make certain he had forgotten nothing, and checked all his work from start to finish. He was perfect and it irritated him, but none the less it had to be. Over the sea, Desmond flying, the port engine cut. He had just changed tanks. I asked him if he was sure he had done it properly and he said 'O.K.', but the intercom was bad and we were losing height – 2,500 feet. I took over, because that was the only way I could see the cocks, and found he had turned the balance on and the tanks off – the opposite to what he should have done. Made a mental note to teach him the petrol system before the next flight and handed the controls back. He was a good pilot, Desmond. I didn't have to watch over him at all.

Route more or less flak-free: some searchlights of course, but none held us and the guns ignored us completely. The moon rose late, in her third quarter. At twenty to eleven I watched her entry from the eastern horizon; at first an orange glow like a monstrous fire in the distance and then, as she rose higher, the gradual fading of her orange mantle until finally she stood naked in the sky.

The visibility was good enough to pick out most of the major pin-points and Taffy was most of the time in the front turret map-reading. The winds not quite as forecast and seemed to be veering inland. Over the hills of the Eifel and beyond map-reading was impossible – no outstanding landmarks – and the Rhine was hidden in mist too, but Taffy came back and Stokey helped him out with bearings. Amazing man, Stokey; he never seems to fail. We came down on E.T.A. knowing at the worst we must be within ten miles of the Daimler Benz Works. There was A.A. in the sky – a lot of it, almost as much as in the Ruhr. All bursting at our height, 8,000 feet, and it was an encouraging sight: they would not bother to defend open country. Seemed to be concentrated in two bunches on either side of us, about ten miles apart. We were almost in the middle. On E.T.A. nothing to pick out except a river, but there were many rivers around and I could not make out which one it was. 'We'll have to fly into the ack-ack and see what they've got to offer. Which one's it going to be? Port or starboard? Come on, Desmond, make up your mind.' 'Port.' 'O.K., port it shall be.'

But there was no sign of the target there either. Flew round and round trying to pin-point something. With the window open the ground stood out fairly clearly, but we could not place anything on the map. Ack-ack seemed to be more concentrated than ever: mostly heavy, and looked like 3·7s: a few searchlights and here and there some tracer. Quite a number of flares too. What with the stick in one hand, a map in the other, trying to speak down the intercom at the same time and flicking the light on every so often to read the map, I had not much time to take evasive action or even to notice where the shells were bursting, but I could see from the corner of my eye they were all around.

At last success; a pin-point on the river. Just what we were looking for. Taff saw it too – eight miles north-east of the target. So we were in the wrong bunch of A.A.

'Desmond, you're slipping.'

A shell burst right in front and some splinters came through the perspex. Then a whole lot more, above, below, behind, everywhere and very close. A searchlight caught us too, but we soon shook that clear. The aircraft was bucketing and rearing about and the bursts were making very strange noises. I shut the window. Desmond seemed to be enjoying it. 'They're predicting us now; looks like a barrage. I'll try and get below it, but we've got to check up that pin-point before we leave the area.' At 2,000 feet the ack-ack left us. I don't know why. Up above at 8,000 feet the ack-ack went on as intense as before, but we were left in peace. 'Everybody must be flying at the same height: why the hell don't they fan out? They've hit someone too – over on the starboard. Do you see it? I thought it was a flare at first, but it's not. I hope to God they managed to jump.'

We opened the bomb-doors, fused the bombs, and Taffy took over. Right over the target at 2,000 feet. It was a gift. The factory was working full blast, we could see it all like daylight. Even cars and lorries. I have never felt such a thrill, and not a gun to stop us. One long stick right across the whole works and we circled round watching results. Two fires straight away, and the incendiaries should start some more: they were burning in one of the sheds, but a stream of tracer started up behind us, so Pike said good-bye in his usual manner, and we left for home in high spirits. Ten hours twenty minutes when we landed. I did not even feel tired. Back at Base they had bombed hell out of the aerodrome. I was thankful not to have been there.

CHAPTER FOUR

ATLANTIC INTERLUDE

Berlin in the air. Only rumours at the moment, but these sort of rumours usually turn out to be true. Taffy running round in a wild state of excitement: says that that is all he asks for, one trip to Berlin. After that they can shoot him down if they like, but just let him have one trip. Well, everybody is the same; after all, Berlin is the reason for most of us joining Bomber Command. But Taffy's hopes were doomed to disappointment, and instead appeared disorganization and bad temper. 'Squadron to move by lunchtime.'

After four hours' frantic packing we took off under sealed orders. Mother and Father were driving up from Oxford to spend a few days near the camp. I was to have lunch with them. Well, that was the luck of the draw. After several stops on the way, all in the space of a week, we found ourselves in Scotland, with an Advanced Base in the wilds to operate from. The weather was perfect: access, too, to the sea and the moors and the warm friendly accent of the Scots, but beyond that nothing to cause rejoicing. No one knew much about our future, except that we were stuck here for an indefinite period.

On the second day I was sent out to Advanced Base and kept there for a long time. I liked the rugged scenery – Desmond did, too, but that was all. Desmond used to go for long walks, sometimes with me but mostly alone, and neither of us had much to say. 'So while they have their cocktail parties and their bathing at Base, we've been left as stooges. Well, as we've said before, to hell with them.' We were not in a good mood. The work was tedious and monotonous. Sea all the time and nothing to attack. I missed the night-flying and the flarepath and going to bed at dawn. I missed, too, the routine we had grown used to and the background of searchlights and shells. Somehow this was a world we did not belong to. There was nothing to rouse the enthusiasm we had known in the past: nothing even to compensate for the hard work. For once we had no regular hours; all day and all night we stood by, waiting for orders to take off; and when the orders came through we might have as little as a quarter of an hour to prepare. In other words, a quarter of an hour to draw our maps, report to Control, work out a flight plan and take off. It was not possible to do it all, so, since at any cost we had to be away on time, we went with only the bare essentials – sometimes as we stood, without parachutes or flying clothing – and worked the flight plan in air. It was good practice in navigation and crew drill, but it made us bad-tempered.

One day orders came through: 'Take off in 25 minutes. Convoy altered course during night; present position unknown: it is essential you find it.' I was sitting in the Crew Room playing patience: Taffy was around too, but the others were nowhere to be seen. We had been operating till 10.30 the night before and were not expecting to be wanted at the worst till after lunch. Still, this was an emergency and we had to go. I went after the maps and charts and navigation stuff, and Taffy flew off to find the crew. Of the 25 minutes, 20 had gone, and still no sign of the others. 'Come on, Taffy, we'll have to go as we are and hope for the best.' 'N' had disappeared, all our kit with it too. Someone must have taken it back, so we took 'P' instead, empty. I started up and taxied out without bothering to run up. As I was turning into wind, Taffy let out a cry: 'Stokey!' Yes, it was Stokey all right, running as hard as he could go. He leapt in and said: 'I haven't got a helmet.'

'Damn that.'

'R's just over there. Won't take a moment to run across.'

'We're late as it is, but I suppose another three minutes won't make any difference.'

And so Stokey went for it.

Two and a half hours later we found the convoy: 34 ships and a large escort. They flashed the O.K. signal and we set about patrolling. The sea was very rough and the weather stormy, closing in all the time. I began to feel restless and stiff, and would have given anything for a biscuit or some coffee, but we had nothing, not even chewing-gum. I missed Desmond too. According to the watch, three more hours' patrolling and then two hours home. 'Damn the sea! I wish there were a few hills or trees or something: anything would do rather than this monotony. My eyes feel as if they are popping out of my head from staring at it. Anyhow, we haven't a hope of seeing a periscope with all these white horses about.' An hour went by; then another. The second was better than the first. I had become resigned, no longer restless, just stiff. Some ack-ack, or something to drop bombs on, would have made all the difference. The visibility grew bad, very bad. I flew down on the water to brighten things up and all but hit a destroyer I had not noticed. From then on it was a question of catch-as-catch-can: pouring rain and visibility about 500 yards. We flew round in circles more or less at mast-height and doing no earthly good in the way of anti-submarine protection.

Stokey suddenly leapt into activity – message from Signals. 'Return to Base, advanced landing-ground weather conditions hopeless for landing.'

'Just as well you brought your helmet after all.'

Forty minutes to go. It was hard work flying in this weather, but at least it was a change from the monotony of the last six hours, and I was thankful not to be on board the convoy. The only real worry was navigation. Taffy was not sure within 20 miles where he was. What with the weather and my flying in circles it was a miracle he was as close as that. Ordinarily 20 miles or so would not have mattered, but with the mountainous, broken coast and clouds on the deck it mattered very much. We tried signalling the leader of the convoy to ask him his position, but had to give it up – visibility too poor.

'It's just occurred to me, Base has no D.F.; advanced landing-ground has, and since Base is surrounded by islands and hills going up to 3,000 feet it must be clear there or they would not divert us. We haven't a hope in hell of making it without D.F. if the clouds are covering the high ground, so I hope they know what they are talking about.'

At 4.30 we set course for home. At 5.30 we were up to 3,000 feet in cloud and still unceasing rain. I tried climbing above it, but there was no sign of daylight, so I came down again. No use trying to go below it either, that was worse still. 'We've been on D.R. now for nearly three hours; if the winds have changed at all we will be miles out. The only thing is to keep above the hills and pray to God there's a gap somewhere.' Taffy nodded his head, but he was not particularly interested. Until we saw land, or at least sea, where he could take a drift, there was nothing for him to do. He was just bored. I was bored, too, and very cold and stiff. I wanted to have a drink and some food and dry clothes, just as the others would be doing at this very moment at Base. It irritated me. At six there were signs of breaks in the clouds. At 6.30 E.T.A. the coast was up. Taffy began to stir and look vaguely out of the window, but there was no definite coastline to cross; just a series of fingers pointing our way and at the moment no gaps in the clouds.

'Come down below the clouds, sir, and I'll get a pinpoint.'

'Don't be bloody stupid, if there's one thing I refuse to do it's kill myself by flying into a hill.'

But half an hour later I took his advice. A small gap, and below it, faintly, the coast. I came down steeply, in a tight left-hand spiral, at all costs keeping clear of the clouds. At 400 feet we were out of cloud: but not for long. Below was a narrow channel and on either side hills disappearing up into the clouds. I opened everything wide and kept the stick right back. I do not suppose a Whitley has ever climbed so steeply before. All the time a curious creepy feeling, because it was impossible to tell which direction, if any, was out to sea and away from the hills.

By 8 o'clock we had carried out a square search which must have covered the area of Base, but nowhere was there any trace of a break.

'This is hopeless, Stokey, you'll have to get a fix and find out if we're anywhere near where we think we are.'

'I can't, haven't brought the book of words.'

'Can you get a homing bearing?'

'Certainly.'

'O.K., we'll home on Advanced Base, and if they try to divert us again, tell them to go to hell. It doesn't matter how low the clouds are there. Once they give us "motors over" we can come right down to nought feet over the lake, and from then on it's easy; but if we don't get there fast we're going to look silly, because we'll run out of gas. Taffy, give me an approximate course to steer while Stokey goes to work.'

Stokey went to work as only he knows how, but it was half an hour before he passed a bearing over, and then it was 80° to the course Taffy had given me. If I had not known Stokey to be the best wireless operator in the Squadron I should have had no idea what to do, for it was hard to believe we were so far out. Nine and a half hours since take-off: no food, no water, not even a helmet to deaden the sound of the engines. But perhaps it was just as well there was nothing to drink, because neither Taffy nor Stokey could have flown in cloud. I thanked God I had practised flying relaxed: without that practice I should have been finished. For the last six hours nothing but instruments: my brain was muddled as it was, and yet I was as happy flying by night as by day. Advanced Base D.F. must have been unprepared for us: they refused to answer Stokey's request except at infrequent intervals. Then, 40 minutes after the first bearing, they gave us a reciprocal.

'Thank God, we must have just passed overhead: it was only ten minutes ago we got the last one. I think I'll come down and find out height of cloud base. No, I won't. I'll keep flying on the reciprocal until we know for certain we're overhead. I still don't want to fly into a hill.'

On we went, and on and on. Five minutes; ten; twenty; thirty; forty. And still no word from Stokey. I knew that if he could not get an answer no one on earth could, so I did not bother to ask him what luck he was having. I did, however, turn through 180° on to the original course. One of the two bearings must be wrong, and I preferred to gamble on it being the reciprocal.

Quarter of an hour later Stokey passed a course through;

more or less the same as the original. So it was just as well I had turned.

Eleven hours. I was already on to the last tank, and there could not be more than 70 minutes' petrol left. Here and there a few gaps, but it was dark, and there was no sign of life below them. Taffy was asleep: he was out of the game now, so I let him sleep on. Stokey said: 'How are you going, Cheese?'

'O.K. I'll outlast the petrol without even trying, but I wish it weren't so bumpy, and I wish the rain would stop coming in.'

Twenty more minutes and a searchlight suddenly lit the clouds beneath us.

'God bless them, they've lit the aerodrome!'

I woke Taffy and came down. Taffy saw what it was and burst into song, but at 600 feet when we broke cloud he stopped abruptly. It was a revolving beacon, not a searchlight, and round about nothing but white horses and an angry sea. For the first time I felt uneasy.

'We can't still be out to sea. God damn it.'

Nobody said anything, and there was no mistaking what we had seen.

'I'm absolutely and hopelessly lost, Stokey, and we're only good for another forty minutes; you'll have to wake that D.F. up even if you have to swear at them in plain language. Do anything; tell them we're short of gas, but don't send an S O S or we'll be court-martialled; it's not urgent enough for that.'

Once more the minutes went by and once more Stokey had nothing to offer. Then suddenly D.F. came through, and this time with bearing after bearing, dozens of them. It came through like Duggie Stewart's tape-machine on Derby Day. 198 – 196 – 200 – 201, all more or less the same. At least we knew we were heading in the right direction, but we still did not know how much further. Twelve hours – it was pitch dark and still rain and cloud. Twelve hours five.

'How much more in the tanks?'

'Six gallons in the port, seventeen in the starboard, according to the gauges.'

'Well, it seems hard to believe, but I don't see what's going to stop us crashing.'

Someone on the ground must have realized what was happening, for Stokey suddenly broke into roars of laughter.

'What's the joke?'

'Look at this; a message from Base: "It's O.K., boys, you're over land; jump."'

Yes, it was funny, we hadn't a parachute between us, and, if we had to come down, the one place we did not want to be was over land. I kicked Taffy on the shin:

'Wake up, damn you! You know you're going to be saved by a last-minute miracle, but don't be so blasé about it.'

But even that did not move him. He smiled serenely like a contented cow. Twelve hours fifteen. The tanks were reading zero or thereabouts, but the engines were still running.

'As soon as the engines cut, lie on the floor, fold your arms over your face and brace your feet for all you're worth. As long as there are no hills below us we ought to get away with it. And, Taffy, take that smirk off your face, it's getting on my nerves.'

Below? Hills, or fields? I wondered which, because it was going to make a big difference. 'I wish to God we had a flare. This forced landing in the dark is pure chance, and I'm not a gambler.'

One minute went by. . . . Stokey's arm on the key and my hands on the controls were the only sign of life, but the engines were still roaring away quite like old times; that red flame on my left. They would never forgive me if I let them down: well, I was not going to. Stokey's arm working away on the key. I could see his thumb, and the curious square shape of his nail. I could see too, three nights ago now, that same thumb twined round a beer-mug, raising it to his lips almost continuously for four hours, and the smile on his face, opening up at everybody in the room, and saying, 'Here's to the war. Here's to the beer.' At the 'Gibraltar', too, the dirtiest, lowest pub you could imagine, but none the less good fun, I saw Stokey leading a riotous sailor twice his own size out of the door. Taffy was there, too, roaring with laughter at whatever was said, whether it was funny or not, and his blue eyes sparkling. Another minute went by, and Taffy settled himself down deeper in his seat. Then suddenly, as if he had sat on a drawing-pin, he leapt to his feet.

'Lights! My God, lights – and an aerodrome at that!'

There it was, right underneath, staring up at us, flarepath and all. I did not wait for a green from Control, but throttled back and came straight in: as long as I kept overhead I could make it even if the engines cut. As the wheels touched down Taffy rolled his eyes and said, 'Gee, I'm hungry.'

The control officer had a curious sense of humour. He said, 'You've made a bloody nuisance of yourself. You said you were short of petrol, so we sent the speedboats out on to the lake, and all the time you had enough to land with.' However, he did apologize for giving us a false reciprocal.

Desmond, on the other hand, looked as if he had come straight out of hell. He had been present when they sent out the message, and knowing we had no parachutes, knowing too it was a serious offence not to carry them, he had suffered agonies wondering whether or not to tell them the truth. He put his arm round my shoulder and said: 'Leonard, ten minutes before you landed the clouds were right down on the deck, and, as you know, they closed in again before you got to the Control Office. If you fell down a cesspit you'd come up with a gold watch and chain round your neck.'

Yes, during the whole of that day and night there was only one break in the clouds. It lasted exactly fifteen minutes, and turned up dead on time as far as we were concerned.

CHAPTER FIVE

THE RUHR

Eleven p.m. somewhere in the Ruhr. Overhead the drone of aircraft circling; on the ground guns and searchlights: hundreds of guns and searchlights, all of them quiet as death, but none the less guns and searchlights, and beside each of them soldiers at action stations, waiting. In all a mighty panorama; and surveying it, a new-born moon. A game worthy of the gods, and at the moment both sides jockeying for position. A stage, too, with players and audience waiting for the curtain to go up. But, before the curtain goes up and the act begins, stop for a while; stop and consider. Overhead a few planes and in them a few bodies. On the ground a few guns, and beside them also a few bodies. The outcome, in essence, is certain. On the ground a few, very few, men and women will lose their lives, a few buildings will be destroyed. In the air, too, a few men will lose their lives, and a few machines be destroyed, possibly. A simple operation without great significance, but think for a while on all that has gone before. To build the aircraft, there has been ship upon ship, bringing iron and steel across the seas. Factories working day after day and year after year, converting raw materials into finished parts. Men and women, called away from their wives and their husbands, labouring at a task they hate and never were meant to perform. On the other side, too, the mighty structure of the Air Force. At the head, the Cabinet has issued a general order based on the dictates of their present policy. From them the order has passed through Air Ministry, the Ministry of Economic Warfare, Bomber Command, Group, the station, and finally to the Squadron itself. With each stage the orders have become more technical and more detailed, and to enable the first general declaration of policy to be interpreted into the orders given to the pilot a countless staff of experts has had to be trained and fed and paid. An equally vast organization, too, has been created to provide a pilot capable of executing these orders, and equally a whole system of supply and maintenance of aircraft, and bombs, and guns, and petrol, and oil, and clothing and countless other tools. And this is but a vision, a small, fleeting vision, of the organization that has been created to enable one pilot to drop one bomb: and when this has been done there is not one member of the whole organization who can so much as lift one finger to influence where the bomb is actually going to fall.

Then, and then only, when these mighty wheels have creaked into motion, is the stage set for the pawns to play their act. And behind the background of Air Vice-Marshals and Cabinet Ministers and blast furnaces and oil-wells and ships and potentates of industry these pawns are very small. Pilot officers and sergeants. Here and there a few squadron leaders and perhaps a Wing Commander or so, but mostly sergeants and pilot officers. Pawns, all of them; gone today and forgotten tomorrow, but, curiously, it is on them that the spotlights are turned. The potentates of industry have built the stage, the Air Vice-Marshals have pulled the curtains apart and in front sit a whole host of reporters, with all the might of a world-wide news service behind them, waiting to flash the picture across the seven seas. The pawns should feel honoured, and, curiously enough, they do. And now they are ready to play.

The advance formation of the attack has arrived. Overhead the air is full of the droning of aircraft, circling and twisting and diving: of dimmed lights, so as better to be able to see the ground: of the rustling of maps and snatches of conversation: of gunners searching the sky for a warning of fighters. And everywhere, eyes. Dozens of pairs of eyes probing and straining, trying to pierce through the darkness to the clue for which they are looking. There is a moon of sorts and no clouds, but even then the ground is not clear. From 8,000 feet prominent landmarks such as lakes and rivers and light-coloured roads stand out, but beyond that not much. The Rhine is the best of them all, but it is over to the west, and, anyway, it is hotly defended. So the eyes will only turn west as a last resort, or when the defences reveal themselves. Back in England, too, there is a quiet air of action. From Air Ministry down to the Squadron, men are standing by, waiting for developments. Some of them have finished their work for the day: it was their responsibility to see the aircraft safely airborne, and now that is done it is their duty to be ready for tomorrow. Others are just getting up, preparing to take over from those who are finished. Others, too, are on duty at the present moment; for the last two hours probably sitting around killing time, but now zero hour is up. At any minute news will come through. Most of it will be 'Mission completed', but there will be other news as well. It may be anything: 'Task abandoned, bombs jettisoned, returning Base'; 'Pilot injured – require medical assistance on landing'; 'Fighter attack developing, will communicate results later.' There may be an SOS, aircraft damaged by flak and unable to maintain height. Perhaps someone will come down in the sea; his position will have to be fixed and the whole rescue organization put into action. If anyone is not awake or makes a mistake five men who could have been saved may be lost. The matter is not a simple one: the aircraft's wireless may be damaged and the only clue of what has happened be a broken, incomplete message. The weather, too, has to be watched. There is a staff of experts who do nothing else but forecast the run of future conditions, but they cannot always be right. Fog may close in suddenly and the aircraft may have to be recalled or diverted to some other part of the country. If it is not done quickly, it may be too late. And in any case, whether an emergency arises or not, the organization has to be ready to receive the crews on their return. Half the task is to drop the bombs, the other half is to know where they have dropped and what are the latest movements of the enemy. Command wants news, not history. And so, while the pawns are still jockeying for position, the brains behind them are stirring and watchful.

On the ground, a semblance of sleep and inactivity, but only a semblance. The watchers on the coast and far inland have heard and guessed and burned their warning along the wires. The sirens have wailed long ago, and the air-raid shelters are full. Inside, the people are quiet: a few nervous, forced voices, but mostly quiet. The Ruhr is a large area. It is attacked some way or another most nights, but what is the target tonight? Essen or Dortmund or Lunen or where? There are many alternatives. The bombers know, the Air Vice-Marshals know, but the people in the shelters do not. Instead, they wonder. It is going to make a big difference. Someone is going to be hurt, and being hit without being able to hit back is an unpleasant business. Already the sound of engines can be heard: louder and louder, then further away, then louder again. And so it goes on, back and forth. It might be anywhere, and it might be any minute. Close your eyes and you will hear what they are saying. 'Adolf, keep still! For God's sake keep still! The creaking of your chair upsets my nerves.'

Up above the ground it is different. The defences are ready: they have work to do, and therefore there is not so much time to reflect. Predictors, sound-locators, shells, fuses. A hundred-and-one things to be done and prepared, and all the time waiting for the order to fire. The night is dark – not very, but dark enough to make map-reading difficult – and it is not a foregone conclusion that the bombers will find their target. The defences are crafty; they are not going to give the position of targets away until they are sure the bombers know where they are. They do not always do that, but that is their policy tonight, and it is a good policy.

In all there is an air of tension, both sides watching each other, like cats, for the first hostile move. Peace reigns over the world, but in the twinkling of an eye this peace may be transformed into a holocaust of steel and gun-powder and fire. The gunners have the drop. They can sit back and watch the movements of the bombers, but they do not know what exactly the bombers are looking for. At any moment one of the attackers may locate his target, and if the defences are not wide awake the boot may be on the other leg. He may drop his bombs undisturbed, and, because he is undisturbed, with accuracy: he may even break out without a single shot to impede him. As soon as his bombs burst every gun will

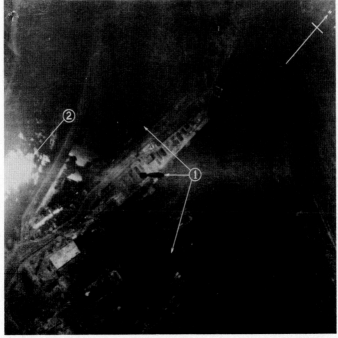

Above Whitley

Below Hamburg during a raid

Above Cologne

Opposite above Hamburg docks

Opposite below Damage to 'N' for Nuts over Cologne

HAMBURG.

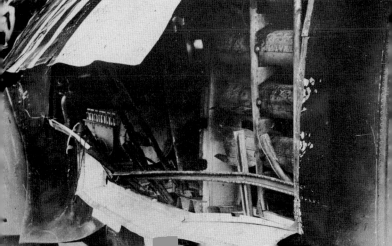

BERLIN. 1123/5.
(WILMERSDORF
STATION)

1.
2.
3.
4.

Above   Whitley cockpit

Opposite above   Berlin: showing tracer, bomb bursts and one searchlight beam

Opposite below   Damage to 'N' for Nuts over Cologne

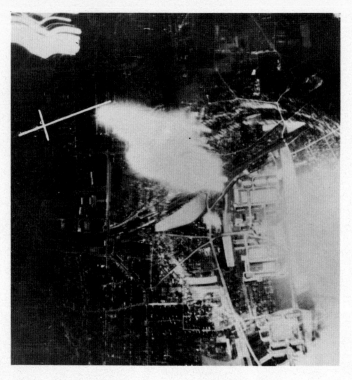

Above   Kassel: aircraft factory on fire during the raid

Opposite above   Halifax. Christopher's 'L' for London

Opposite below   From left to right: Revs, Brown, Taffy, Gutteridge, Self, Hares, Jacko, Weldon

Above   Halifax cockpit

Opposite   Flak

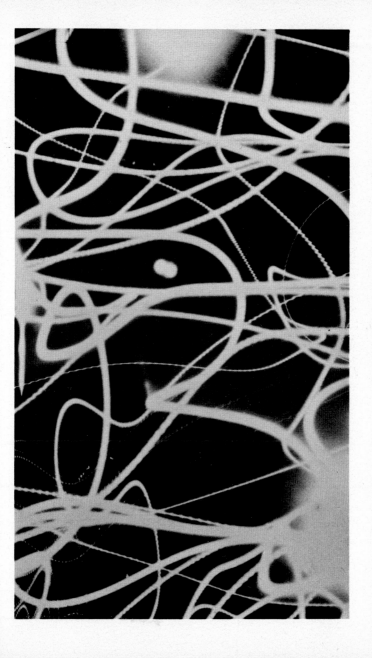

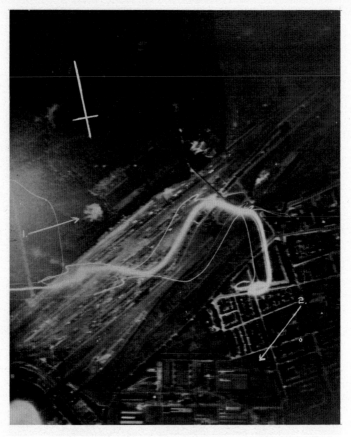

Above   Karlsruhe: we brought back a good photograph

Opposite above   Cologne: as it used to be

Opposite below.   *Back row* Ground crew. We never once failed to
take off or turned back through engine trouble
Front row Crock, Martin, Henry, Self, Jock, Paddy, Revs

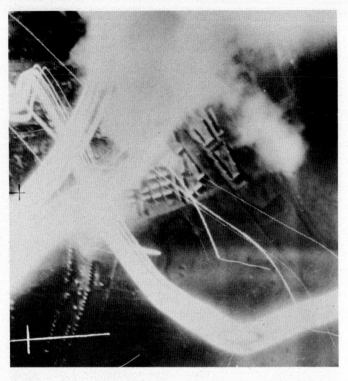

Above   Warnemünde during the heavy raid. Fires and smoke clearly visible

Opposite   Christopher's Halifax. 'L' for London. Note camouflage effect on starboard wing

Above Berlin: (1) Willy's bombs bursting on the central meat market; (3) gunflashes

Opposite Paddy, Martin, Henry. 'Running up' in snow

Halifax discarding its load. Photograph taken of the Squadron
Commander over the battleship in daylight

crash into action, but the sky is full of aircraft, all at different heights and speeds and courses. If the first bombs find their mark, every bomb-sight in the sky will converge overhead, because that is what the eyes behind the bomb-sights have been straining to see. As soon as they see it, the air of quiet tension will disappear. The crews will jump into action. 'Bomb-doors open. Bombs fused. Left, left; steady. Bombs gone.' It may all take a few seconds: it may even take five minutes, but in any case it will not take very long, and then overhead there will be silence until the next wave of attackers arrives. The defences will not have long in which to wreak their vengeance.

On the ground the action will be faster still and more furious. Once it was a scattered, uneven drone in the skies and the men on the predictors cautious: taking their time and merely checking and rechecking their readings. An air of waiting too. Close your eyes again, and you will hear their conversation: 'Where are they going?' 'They've passed over.' 'They're going away.' 'Perhaps Frankfurt.' 'No, he's turning round.' 'He's coming back. He's circling: losing height.' 'He's coming our way now, along the railway line. In a few moments he'll be right overhead.' 'There are others, too, from the west, but they are higher.' 'Some from the north now; and the north-east.' 'Donnerwetter, the sky is full of them: louder and louder. Every minute closer.' 'They are coming to us.' 'Why should it be us? Last night it was us too.' 'And we can't stop them.' 'Not with guns.' 'Some of them we can hit, if we are lucky, but that doesn't make any difference.' 'There are too many of them, and they are not afraid.' 'Even if we do hit them, the bombs will still fall.' 'Shoot! Why in heaven's name don't they tell us to shoot? They sit there in control in a bomb-proof shelter and tell us to hold our fire, but they don't know what it means out here in the open, waiting, just waiting for the bombs to fall.' 'Perhaps this is the order now.' 'Battery Number 3? Yes, battery commander speaking. I can't hear you; speak louder. Yes, I know: he's overhead now. 1,550 metres. There are many others too, higher up. Leave them? But if we don't fire at them they will hit us.' 'It doesn't matter, there are too many for accurate prediction. Take the one lower down, A78. Every battery in the group will fire on him, and keep firing till he is brought down. At all costs leave the others alone. We have shot nothing down for three nights. This time we have got to be successful, so concentrate on A78. He is coming very low and very slow. Soon he will be in range of all batteries, even machine-guns. As soon as the order to fire is given the searchlights will light up, all of them, and keep him illuminated. You will be able to fire by sight, not by sound-location. When his course is ascertained all light anti-aircraft units will lay a simultaneous curtain ahead of him so that he must fly through it to reach the target. We have many guns – 630, and an average of 23 shells a minute: we can't miss him.'

'Did you hear that? Adolf, did you hear that? A78. We're going to bring him down. The fool, he thinks we are asleep or he wouldn't dare come so low.'

'Battery No. 3. Square 135. He will be in square 135, height 920 metres, at zero hour. All units will fill square 135. Zero hour 60 seconds from signal. Stand by ... 5 ... 4 ... 3 ... 2 ... 1 ... UP!'

'Square 135. Fuse 3.3. Stand by. 50 ... 30 ... 15 ... 10 ... 5 ... 4 ... 3 ... 2 ... 1 ... FIRE!'

'O.K., got it. Do you see it, Taffy? Absolutely perfect. I can even see the bridge over the southern end. Looks like a horseshoe. I'll fly round over the top for a while until you've worked out course and E.T.A. to Lunen. Get it exact to the second and then time it by stop-watch. I'm going to fly dead straight and level. There's no flak at all at the moment: I'll try to get through before they open. If we do, it will be a walkover – no clouds and enough moon to show the ground up. Stokey, stand by to drop a flare. I don't suppose we'll need one, but we might. Height will be about 3,000: minimum fuse-setting.'

'Do you want a flare, sir?'

'No, not now. I'll let you know when. Just stand by, and take a parachute with you: you're the wrong side of the petrol tank.'

'Never have yet. Waste of energy.'

'O.K., don't blame me. Got that course yet, Taffy?'

'Certainly. 349: 12 minutes dead.'

'O.K. Turning on. We're right over the lake; I'm turning on. Now!'

'Okidoke, sir. It's a cinch.'

'Don't go to sleep just because we've got this pin-point. Keep your eyes glued on the map. And, Desmond, go forward, open the escape-hatch and stick your head out. We're going to make damn' sure what part of the target the bombs hit. They seem to think our two months' absence has caused us to forget what little we ever knew, and they're wrong; hopelessly, ridiculously wrong, but they might as well know it.'

For a while, silence. Taffy, in the nose, quietly adjusting himself to his liking, checking up to make certain there is nothing left out. He is lying prone on his stomach, methodically testing switches and lights and bomb-sight settings. Desmond has the escape-hatch open and is kneeling over the hole, his hands wedged against the floor on the other side, peering out. I think Taffy must have accidentally kicked him on the back of the head, because he has jumped up suddenly and is swearing to himself. He looks at me, roars with laughter and kneels down again.

'Strangely quiet tonight. I've never seen the Ruhr like this before. Not a single gun or even a searchlight. I wonder what's going on. Maybe they've run out of ammunition.'

'Yes, and maybe they're waiting for some sucker to fly straight and level long enough so that they can't miss him.'

'What's the railway on the starboard, Taffy? Are you O.K. on the map?'

'Certainly. We're right dead on track and very nearly there. Target should be coming up any moment. Shall I bomb if I get a good sight?'

'No, certainly not. We're going to identify it first and make damn' sure there's no mistake. Anyway, we're too high.'

'Are you going to need a flare?'

'No, I don't think so, but you'd better stay there just in case. Revs, are you O.K. in the tail?'

'Fine, Captain, but I don't think much of these German defences.'

'What's that below, Taffy? Looks mighty like the target to me.'

'Yes, it is, but I'm just checking up to make dead sure, like you said I had to.'

'Good show. Well, I'll turn off west, lose height, and come in on a heading 090. The ack-ack's still as quiet as death. I doubt it lasts much longer, but we'll try and make it, anyway.'

I circle once and turn off. What a pity it isn't possible to bomb from where we are, without having to fly away and come in again! At 5,000 feet I turn left about and head on to 090. Bomb-doors open, bombs fused, and Taffy adjusting his bearings before taking over.

'If your aiming's bad, I'll break your neck. It's a sitting target, a mile long by half a mile wide, the visibility's perfect, and even though you have to do six dummy runs you've got to hit it.'

Desmond said he was getting cold, and not to throw the aeroplane about too much in case he fell out.

'Holy Moses, did you see that?'

On the ground, like a sheet of summer lightning, rippled a wave of angry, orange flashes. Gunfire.

'I hope it's not us they have in mind.'

The last gun closed down, the last searchlight faded out, and overhead the drone of aircraft disappeared gradually into the distance. The play was over: the tension had come and risen and finally exploded in a fury of fire and steel, and now, 55 minutes later, that too was gone. In its place was an air of relief and quiet. Desmond passed his hand over his face, muttered silently to himself and reached for a flask of coffee with a hand that was streaming with perspiration. Stokey came back from the flare-chute, his face flushed like a beet-root, and away on the starboard quarter a few searchlights roamed idly round the sky. I watched them for a moment and thought how good it was to drink canteen coffee in peace. The gyro was 20° out of true with the compass: I reset

84

it and tried to unstick my back from my shirt. Taffy came grinning out of the front turret, carrying a handful of twisted metal that had once been a bomb-sight. Desmond looked down at him and suddenly began to roar with laughter. I laughed too, because, thinking back on it, I saw that it was funny. The flashes on the ground, that first thundering barrage, Desmond slamming the hatch shut because from the way the aircraft was rocketing about he nearly fell out, Taffy shrieking optimistically at me to follow the railway line, and, although even at 1,000 feet it was cold, sweat pouring off my face from start to finish. Yes, now it was all over, it was funny to look back on, and a flood of memories swept through my mind. The crash of shells, the venom of the light tracer, the glare of the searchlights. *They* weren't particularly funny; it was our reactions and the expressions on our faces: the way we edged hopefully away each time a shower of splinters came rattling through the fuselage. Then our shouting and excitement against the noise from outside, until speech was almost unintelligible.

A garbled snatch of conversation, just after we dropped the first stick of bombs, echoed through my ears.

'Bombs gone.'

Then almost immediately:

'Bomb-sight too.'

'Bomb-sight too what?'

'Got it, got it: absolutely magnificent. Got it slap in the middle.'

'Got what? For God's sake, man, pull yourself together: you're not George Robey, you know. Desmond, go and see what's the matter with Taffy. He's probably bumped his head on the perspex.'

'It's not Taffy, Captain, it's me.'

'Who the hell's me?'

'It's O.K., Cap, it's only a splinter: carry on.'

'Thanks very much.'

'Shall I open up?'

'Open up what? Has everybody gone mad on this ship, or is it me?'

'Who are you?'

'Rear gunner speaking.'

'Bomb-sight's disappeared, Captain.'

'What the hell's the bomb-sight got to do with the rear gunner?'

'It's not the rear gunner, it's Taffy.'

'Well, I'll put you on a charge when we get back.'

'When!'

From the fuselage came an ear-splitting crack, presumably an explosive shell. The communicating-door under the petrol-tank banged open, and a scarlet face popped out. Stokey. He looked around, and having come to the conclusion that everything was under control tapped his head significantly and shot back again like a rabbit bolting out of a hole and seeing a man with a gun standing just outside.

In the peaceful Dutch air the explanation was simple. Taffy was trying to say the bomb-sight was hit and that he had a splinter in his face. Rear gunner had got excited because he had seen the bombs hit the target and he wanted to open up with his guns on the defences, and Stokey, in spite of his principles, was on the point of fetching his parachute.

Desmond's laughter died away and the memories faded. As the minutes ticked silently by we settled down to doze and to dream. The coast came, England came, and half an hour before dawn we landed. There were over a hundred holes in the aircraft. I stood by the hatch watching the others jump out, and thought: 'They haven't said anything, but if any of them had been hurt it would have been entirely my fault; they told me not to monkey around with the Ruhr.' Last of all out of the hatch came a long, lanky man with a huge jaw. Revs his name: our new rear gunner and his first trip. I walked up to him apologetically, not quite knowing what to say. He stretched his shoulder-blades contentedly, and a lazy smile spread slowly between his long ears.

'At last I can die happy: I know what it means to see a factory blow sky-high.'

He could not have known it was by sheer luck that we passed dead over the target.

CHAPTER SIX

COLOGNE

'Good morning, Colonel.'

'Good morning to you. Did you find the target?'

'No, the clouds were there before us.'

'That's what the others said. Did you bring your bombs back?'

'No, certainly not. Cologne.'

'Did you go in at a reasonable height for a change?'

'No: 8,000, as I was told to.'

'Any holes?'

'A few, not many.'

'Yes, you see, it's much better to go in high, isn't it?'

'I don't think so at all, but maybe you're right.'

'Get any results from the flares? Group want to know.'

'Yes, we got some results, but not quite what they wanted.'

'You'll send in a report then, will you? Nobody injured, I suppose?'

'Yes, wireless operator.'

'Stokey?'

'No, he wasn't able to come. Davy, a brand-new one: his first trip.'

'Serious?'

'Yes, I'm afraid so. It will be touch-and-go whether they save him. Anyway, he's blind.'

'Well, you'd better go and get some sleep. You look tired. We heard nothing from you from start to finish. We thought maybe something had happened to you.'

'Wireless U.S. I don't think I want to sleep, but I could use some food. Come on, Desmond; come on, Revs. Good night, Taffy. And, Taffy . . .'

'Yes, sir?'

'Thanks.'

'Damn you, Taffy! Damn you – damn you, and again damn you! Look, for God's sake, this isn't a game. This ack-ack's getting hot. We can't hang around here for ever. What's more, the cloud's closing in all the time, and if you're not quick we're not going to see anything at all. . . . Answer me, will you? Answer me, damn you! The moon's absolutely full, the ground's quite clear, and I've never seen the Rhine stand out so well in all my life; if you can't pin-point yourself tonight, you'd better give up navigation and take up tiddley-winks. Desmond, go and see what's the matter with him. If he's still in full possession of his senses, and merely can't get his position, grab the map from him, and we'll do the map-reading ourselves. Got that?'

'Yep.'

'O.K. in the tail, Revs? . . . Revs! . . . Rear gunner!'

'Rear gunner speaking.'

'Captain here. Can't you hear me very well?'

'Very faint and indistinct.'

'Listen hard, then. I've just seen a fighter; on the port beam, flying in the opposite direction. It's very bright, so keep a good look-out. He's mixed up in his own ack-ack. I hope he gets himself shot down. Keep your eyes on these shell-bursts too: they're pretty accurate tonight.'

'Right you are, Captain.'

'Wireless op.'

'Wireless op speaking, sir.'

'Hullo, Davy. You O.K. there?'

'Everything O.K., Captain.'

'Good show. I'm sorry there's so much shouting going on: navigator's gone to sleep or something. Hang on to that flare till I let you know. Height the same – 9,000: we won't need a recco. flare, so you can concentrate entirely on the special one. Don't drop it or explode it, or anything: it's worth an incredible number of candle-power.'

'O.K., Captain, standing by.'

Desmond at last came back: he banged his head on the instrument-panel and started muttering to himself in his usual manner. Very slowly and deliberately he settled down on the step, wriggled about till he was quite comfortable and then plugged in to the intercom.

'Well, what's the verdict?'

'Intercom must be U.S., or else it's his helmet. He says he's been shouting at you for the last twenty minutes and wants to know if you're still here – says you won't answer and keep on turning the opposite way to which he tells you. He knows exactly where you are, and he's been screaming his head off because you won't lead him over the target.'

'Where are we?'

'Twelve miles north: between Wesseling and Cologne.'

'O.K., I'll turn south.'

'No, it's too late: the target's covered by cloud.'

'Hell! It's no use hanging around trying to get below it, the whole Rhine will be covered in a moment. There must be the hell of a wind.'

'North-west: 80 miles an hour. Taffy's worked it out.'

'We'll go for Cologne then: I shall be able to find that myself and make a run-up more or less in the right direction. Go and tell Taffy, will you? Tell him to aim for the marshalling yard. As soon as we're heading on approximately, he's to show which way to turn by kicking his feet. You'll have to pass on to me which foot he's kicking. O.K.?'

'Yes, O.K.'

'Oh, Desmond . . .'

'Yes?'

'Tell him I've been swearing at him, but I didn't know what the trouble was and I'm sorry.'

'Right you are.'

'About five minutes, Dav, and we'll want your flare. Sorry you've had so long on your ownsome.'

'O.K., sir.'

'I'll fly up the east bank, Desmond, then we can bomb into wind and be heading more or less for home at the same time. The ack-ack's a bit weaker now. They're concentrating on someone else. D'you see him? Over to port and below us, just west of the river. Hell, they're giving him all they've got: he'll never get out of those searchlights, even though the moon is so bright. I wonder who it is: not Jimmy, I hope. He said he wanted to go in low. Keep your eyes open for fighters, Revs: we'll watch the rest. I think they've got him. Yes, they have: his port wing's on fire. So's his starboard. He still seems to be under control, though. Must be either his tanks or his engines. He's flying straight, but losing height fast. Keep a look-out for parachutes: they should have plenty of time to jump. In fact, I think they must have jumped already: the guns have stopped firing at them.'

'I think there's a fighter behind, Captain.'

'O.K., keep your eye on it and let me know if he closes in.'

'I've lost him now. I think he can't have seen us.'

'We're almost up to Cologne now. Is Taffy ready, Desmond?'

'Yes, he's putting his settings on the bomb-sight. Bombs are fused and bomb-doors open.'

'Right. I'm turning on now. I can't see the ground ahead, only below, so it will be a very approximate heading. Let Taffy know, will you?'

'Yes, O.K., he's caught on. Left, hard left. The ack-ack's stopped altogether: not a sign of a gun or a searchlight anywhere.'

'What's the time?'

'One-thirty-five.'

'Our time's up ten minutes ago: we're probably the only aircraft here.'

'The guns may think we've dropped our bombs and are on our way home, and therefore have given up worrying about us.'

'Don't be a complete half-wit; we've met this game before – it's a trap. I'd like to know exactly how, but I'll lay you any odds you like it's a trap; probably fighters.'

'Left, left; further still, about 20 degrees.'

And still silence from the guns; a nasty creepy feeling. I felt a curious, almost heavy, presentiment. Stupid, but I could not seem to fight it back.

'Right a little. Steady.'

'What the hell are those guns playing at? It's almost uncanny.'

'Look out! Turn quick. Over to . . .'

The explosion kicked my mind back a quarter of a century. Down. Down. We're going down. I can feel the rush of air. We are going so very fast – 200, 300, 400 miles an hour. I don't know, but who on earth would? Alice in Wonderland didn't, did she? She only knew she was going down. Why do my eyes hurt so much? God, I can't see! Everything is black, black as a rook. No, raven, of course. Yes, raven, not rook. I must be blind. I've always wanted to know what it's like to be blind, and now I know. The funny thing is that it doesn't really seem any different, except merely that I can't see: there must be more to it than that. I suppose it's just that I've not got used to it yet. No! Good lord, how stupid I am! I'm not blind at all! It's that terrible flash. Yes, I'm beginning to remember now. Just in front of me. A terrible bright yellow flash. It seemed to split my eyes right open, right round to the back of my head. Yes, a bright flash like that blinds you for a bit, but after a few minutes you can see again. Minutes? Or should it be seconds? I don't know. I can't seem to be able to work anything out properly: probably I'm getting tired. No, it must be minutes, because it's so long ago since it all happened. Like coming out of a lighted room into the dark.

And the noise. Yes, what a noise! It felt as though it broke every bone in my body. But I don't think it can have; I feel more or less all right. A bit peculiar, that's all. What is it? I know, I feel sick. More at heart than anything, but it's in my stomach. We've got to jump. Jump? Yes, jump. I've never jumped in my life. I've often wanted to, but I never have. Now I've got to. It's not quite the same, though. If I was going to jump, I wanted to do it in my own good time, not in Jerry's time. I've often thought about this moment, and wondered whether it would be possible to do everything in time. Unplug yourself, wind the trimmer-tab back, climb out of the seat, down into the well, and get your parachute.

God knows where my parachute is now. I hurled it somewhere in the nose when I got in, but I haven't seen it since. There were one or two there some time ago, but goodness only knows if any of them were mine. Yes, I've thought about all that from time to time, but I've always said, 'Oh, well, you won't think anything to it, because if the situation arises where you've got to jump, you'll be so bloody glad to get out you won't give a damn about anything else,' but now I know how foolish I was. The thought of jumping is worse than anything. I'd rather stay here and hope for the best. If this is the end, if there is to be no more briefing, no more 'Good morning, Colonel', no more letters from Mother, or blinds in the 'Half Moon', or 'phone calls from Maxine, I've got to have more time to think it over. An incident so big in my life can't just come and pass and disappear like that: it doesn't somehow seem right. Right? Well, that's peculiar, because it doesn't feel right at all. In fact, it feels wrong. What the hell is it? I can't think, but I know something is wrong. Just like that first flight with Desmond. I knew something was wrong then – the red and green lights. Oh, I know what it is. How stupid! Everything feels stupid just now. Yes, the control column. It's gone. My hands aren't holding it: they're resting loose on my thighs. They shouldn't be: they should be holding the control column. It can't have disappeared altogether. I'll have a look for it. Ah, here it is. Yes, I've got it. What a difference that makes! I feel like a new man altogether. What a curious life this is! Pull back the stick and we won't go down any more. I don't know, though – we're still going down very fast. I know it's fast because the wind is singing past my ears. Down. Why always down? Something to do with rain, isn't it? King Lear, Hamlet, Richard II – yes, Richard, I think it is. No, I'm not sure even of that; it's so long since I read Shakespeare.

'Have you dropped the bombs?'

What on earth made me say that? I wasn't thinking of bombs or anything like them. I didn't even mean to say it: it just slipped out. Nobody seems to answer: I don't suppose anybody's left alive. Anyway, as far as the bombs go, it doesn't matter very much. If we're going to crash, the bombs may as well stay with us, and if we aren't going to crash, we may as well drop them some place. What's making me cough? I haven't got a cold, have I? No, I'm sure I haven't. Not a few moments ago I hadn't. If I go on coughing I'll be able to get some Allenbury's blackcurrant pastilles – that'll be fun. It's getting worse, though – much worse. My eyes are smarting too. What a foul smell! Bitter, like that day in the shelter when they bombed the aerodrome. If it goes on much longer I won't be able to breathe. I need a towel soaked in water. 'Desmond get me a towel.' No, of course, Desmond isn't there. I wonder what's happened to him. Oxygen mask! That's the thing: oxygen mask. Where is it? Hanging from my neck somewhere, but where? Good, I've got it. Quick, man, quick, before it's too late. No, not too quick. Something about cooks and spoiling the broth. No, it's not that. More haste, less speed. Hold your breath: that's the way. Now find the press stud. Take your gloves off: you can't clip it on while you're wearing gloves. That's got it. Oh, God, what a blessed relief! What a blessed relief! I shall never go without my gas mask again!

'Have you dropped the bombs yet?'

Nobody seems to answer. Funny, that; surely there must be someone there. Desmond wouldn't have gone off without saying cheerio. No, I'm wrong; somebody's speaking. What's he saying? I can't quite make it out. Yes, I can.

'I've been hit. I've been hit.'

I wonder who it is. I can't recognize the voice and he doesn't say his name. It must be coming from the front, not the back. Something awful has happened at the back. I don't quite know what, but most of the explosion seemed to come from behind. First of all it was in front, that terrible bright flash. And then almost immediately afterwards a much bigger explosion from behind my back. There can't possibly be anyone left alive there: so it must be coming from the nose. What shall I say? I can't think of anything. It doesn't really matter much: not at the moment. We've got to stop going down first. What an awful thing to think – that it doesn't matter much. But I can't help it. There's nothing I can do anyway, and, whether I like it or not, I did think it. I suppose the answer is that when you're in a spot you think of yourself first.

The smoke cleared, and like a ray of sunshine my eyesight came back. I blinked once or twice, perhaps; I don't know.

Anyway, I could see quite well. I looked at the altimeter: 5,000 feet. Plenty of height, much more than I would have thought possible. Somehow we seemed to have been diving for ages and ages, and we were still diving now. The instruments were all haywire; they did not make sense however you looked at them. They must have been shot away behind the panel. Awkward. But when we levelled out and ceased diving they began slowly to come back to normal, so probably they were intact after all. I rubbed my forehead between my eyes, and started to take stock of the damage. First of all, the engines and the wings. Perhaps a few pieces of twisted burned metal: not more. They must have borne the brunt of the explosion. I looked out, and, like the man who saw the table slide slowly of its own accord across the floor, sat frozen to my seat. They were running; both of them. Running as they've always run before. Two long protruding noses, almost Jewish, and a defiant roar. My ears became suddenly unblocked, and into them poured the music of this defiant roar. Why was it I hadn't heard it before? And how, oh how could I doubt their trust? Perhaps for a while I had lost possession of my senses.

Something was stirring. I looked up and saw there was a figure standing in the well, staring at me. The lights had fused. In the half darkness of the moon it was a grotesque figure, leaning drunkenly on an enormous pair of arms, and a pair of wide, gaping eyes, and face and shoulders streaming with blood. Who or what it was, God only knows. I didn't. I tried to work things out, but somehow had to give up. The only association I could make was with the voice that said: 'I've been hit. I've been hit.' And all the time we were staring into each other's eyes. Suddenly he looked away, down the fuselage, and uttered a strangled cry:

'Fire! The tank's on fire!'

'Well, put it out then.'

At last, thank God, I regained my senses. I don't think the figure in the well heard what I said: before I had finished speaking he had disappeared on his hands and knees down the fuselage, where the petrol tank was. And then for a long while I was left in solitude.

We were flying straight and level, at least more or less so, but something, somewhere, was radically wrong. The aircraft was wallowing and flopping around like a small boat on a gentle swell, and the controls felt as though they had come unstuck. I looked at the engines with a song in my heart, and then back at the instruments. It was incredible, but nowhere on any of the gauges was there a sign of trouble. I could hardly believe my eyes. The compass, I noticed, was steady; so were the rest of the flying instruments. They couldn't have been damaged, then, after all. I set about synchronizing the gyro with the compass, for it was hopelessly out, and only then did I realize the truth. What a fool! What an incredible, bloody fool! We were flying due east, back into Germany, and down an eighty-mile-an-hour wind at that! Of all the times to forget an elementary principle! Without thinking what I was doing, I pulled the stick hard over, and again I cursed myself for being a fool. The port wing dropped, the nose reared up, and only just in time I stopped her spinning. From then on I treated the controls as though they were made of putty, and it was three minutes before we were back on a westerly course.

The thought of what I had done made me sweat, and that was comforting, because if I was capable of sweat there could not be overmuch wrong. But this comfort did not last long, and the smile came off my face. I began to notice the sweat was all on my back and not my front. What's more, my back was getting hotter and hotter all the time. By this time I was prepared to believe anything, but this was definitely not normal. I screwed my head round, and what I saw forced a quiet, unwanted curse from my lips. Thick, black, oily smoke, pouring out from beneath the petrol tank, and in the background red gashes of fire.

I did not stay looking long, for on the port and ahead of us a barrage of shells came up. They were bursting in bunches of twenty or thirty, like that Saturday over the Ruhr, only this time they seemed to make more noise, because the hatch above my head was missing and all around the perspex was torn. Instinctively I started to take evasive action, but remembered just in time. If only I knew what was wrong with the controls it would make it easier. It felt as though the cables were hanging on by a thread, but I could not be certain. Anyway, it was better to take the shells than settle everything by pulling the controls off. So I flew straight and level. A searchlight picked us up, then a lot more, and almost immediately a rattle of splinters came through the fuselage somewhere behind me. I switched on the microphone and started speaking, but no one answered. The heat seemed no worse, but I did not look round any more. Somehow, I could not take my eyes off the shells. On the floor beside me was a parachute. It was not mine. In the nose there were two others, and there was no one except me this side of the petrol tank. What if they could not put the fire out? They would never get past the tank again. I found I was clutching the control column like a drowning man at a straw, and cursed myself. Tried to fix my mind on things that mattered, but it was elusive. I could not hold it down. Curious visions again. Damn them: it's as bad as being drunk. A grotesque figure in the well. Who on earth was it? I'm sure it can't have been the voice that said 'I've been hit,' because the intercom in the front was U.S. Good lord, he's come back! I'll fix him this time. In fact I'll ask him straight who he is. I looked up at his face, but I did not have to ask him his name.

'Hello, Desmond. Where you been hiding?'

'Can you keep her in the air?'

'What do you think?'

'That's all I wanted to know.'

'What about the fire?'

'If you can keep her going another five minutes, we'll have it under control.'

They were long, those five minutes, very long, but they got the fire out. Taffy was the first to come back: bleeding and glistening, but grinning all over his face.

'What's the verdict?'

But all he did was roar with laughter. Infectious. I roared with laughter too, and felt better: much better.

'What about the bombs? Have we still got them?'

'Certainly.'

'Well, we'd better go find Cologne.'

Taffy looked back over my shoulder, shouted out 'Jesus!' and dashed off down the fuselage. What he went to do I don't know. I only know there was, for a while, a confusion of cries and noise and violent movement, and then Taffy came back and disappeared into the front turret. The shells were still as fierce as ever, but now that there had been diversion it was not quite so bad. Someone flopped down beside me. I looked up. He was squatting on the step, his head down below his knees and his arms covering his face. I leant across and pulled him gently back. Pray God I may never see such a sight again. Instead of a face, a black, crusted mask streaked with blood, and instead of eyes, two vivid, scarlet pools.

'I'm going blind, sir: I'm going blind!'

I didn't say anything: I could not have if I had wanted to. He was still speaking, but too softly for me to hear what it was. I leaned right across so as better to hear. The plane gave a lurch, and I fell almost on top of him. He cried out and once more buried his face below his knees. Because I could not stand it, I sat forward over the instruments and tried to think of something else, but it was not much good. Then suddenly he struggled to his knees and said:

'I haven't let you down, have I, sir? I haven't let you down, have I? I must get back to the wireless. I've got to get back. You want a fix, don't you, sir? Will you put the light on, please, so that I can see?'

So it was Davy. Davy: his very first trip. Someone came forward and very gently picked him up. Then came Desmond. He sat down beside me and held out his hand. I took it in both of mine and looked deep into his smiling blue eyes.

'Everything's under control.'

'God bless you, Desmond.' Never have I said anything with such feeling. 'What about Davy? Is he going to die?'

'He's O.K. Revs is looking after him.'

'Thank God. Tell me the worst. What's the damage?'

'Pretty bad.'

'Will she hold?'

'I don't know. About evens I should say. The whole of the port fuselage is torn: there's only the starboard holding.'

'How about the controls?'

'I don't know. They look all right, but it's difficult to tell. Shall I go and look more carefully?'

'No, it makes no odds. We're going to make a break for it however bad they are. If they're damaged, I think I'd rather not know. If this ack-ack doesn't stop soon I shall lose control of myself, Desmond. I can stand all the rest, but this I can't. They've got us stone cold. We can't turn, and we can't dive, and we can't alter speed, and it's only their bad shooting that will—'

A staccato crack, and Desmond covered his face.

'Desmond, Desmond! Are you all right?'

'Yes, sure.'

'You're bleeding.'

'That's nothing. A bit of perspex, probably: the splinter missed me. Taffy's signalling. Have you still got the bombs or something?'

'Yes. Which way?'

'Right. Hard right. Go on, much further.'

'Tell him to shut up. What the hell does he think this is? A Spitfire?'

We went on like this for some time. Turning all the time, very gently, but none the less turning, and always to the right. Then at last the bombs went. I felt the kick as they left the aircraft. Desmond stood up and went back to Revs and Davy.

'Where was it?'

'Cologne.'

Yes, there was the Rhine right beneath us. I recognized the wide curve just south of the town. What a long way we must have flown back into Germany, and all through my carelessness. Then Taffy came back. He jerked his thumbs and laughed, but his face looked a little drawn.

'What luck?'

'Wizard. In the middle of the yard.'

'Fair enough. Go and work me out a course for home, will you? I'm flying 310: more or less right.'

He looked me full between the eyes. 'Shall we make it, sir?'

'Why, of course, Taffy.' Never have I seen such a genuine look of relief over anyone's face. I thought: 'He's a trusting soul, Taffy. I hope no one ever takes advantage of it, because if they do he'll fall with an awful bump.'

'Have you got the chart, sir?'

'No. Why, isn't it there?'

'No, only the bottom end. It must have blown out of the hatch or got burnt or something. The log has gone, too.'

'Can you piece the quarter-inch maps together and lay off an approximate course?'

'No, most of them are missing, too. I've only got England and the target area.'

'Hell! Try to remember what our course in was. You've got the wind, haven't you? It must still be set on the C.S.C., unless you've lost that, too.'

'No, I've got that, but I've no idea of our course in.'

'Nor have I. Hang on, though: I'll get it in a moment. If only I could get my brain working again! Yes, I know – 140. It may have been 150, but 140 will do. All that remains is to knock off the wind, find the track, apply the wind again to the reciprocal and we've got an approximate course. Do your best, will you? The distance beats me altogether, though. About 150 to the coast I should say.'

'O.K., sir.'

But that was as far as he got. He had been using a C.S.C. every day of his life for nearly two years, and therefore he knew the intrument like his own hand, but this time he could make nothing of it. He sat for perhaps ten minutes staring at it blankly and then gave it up.

'O.K., Taffy, to hell with it. We'll continue on 310. It won't be far out.'

Desmond came and sat beside me.

'How's it going?'

'Not so bad. What about Davy?'

'I've fixed him up best I can. Went and got the first-aid kit and put some Tannafax on. Seems to have relieved the pain quite a bit.'

'Give him some morphia.'

'He won't have it. Insists on getting back to the set, and we had to let him go to quieten him down. He's been working away for the last twenty minutes.'

'But he can't see.'

'I know. He calls out the dial settings, Revs does his best to fix them and then guides Davy's hands to the key. They haven't got anything through yet, though. I think the set must be U.S.'

'Good God, man, we don't need wireless as bad as that! We'll get back somehow, even though we have to land in Hyde Park.'

'I know, but it only makes it worse trying to stop him. How d'you feel yourself?'

'O.K. It's just these guns that get on my nerves. The first shock took all my strength, and I didn't have time to muster enough will-power to keep my mind off the shells. You know how it is, if you suddenly call on all the concentration you've got, you're left defenceless, like putting a hedgehog on its back, and until you get yourself on your feet again you've got to take whatever comes along. Still, I've built my reserve up again now, and I'm O.K. They can go on firing as much as they like. Actually they're slowing down quite a lot: we should be out of range before very long.'

'Yes, I felt much the same, but while I was down by the fire and looking after Davy I didn't mind so much. The cold's the worst of the lot.'

'Yes, it's all these gaps in the roof. The temperature's actually only minus 16, but it's the draught. My feet are frozen stiff. It must be hell for Davy. Can you manage to get him out of the draught somewhere?'

'There is nowhere. The best place is where he is, on the set.'

Slowly, one by one, the guns faded out, and slowly too we settled down to a stretch of ordinary, commonplace flying. Above, the moon was high in the heavens and very bright: below stretched a blanket of billowing white clouds. The engines were still roaring the same steady, triumphant roar: the aircraft was still wallowing and rearing – sometimes, I thought, a little more agitatedly, sometimes a little steadier. I could not make up my mind which. For the most part inside the aeroplane there was silence.

'Desmond, have Revs come up here: I want to talk to him.'

He came and squatted beside me, the same calm, smiling Revs. He jerked his jaw and said, 'Magnificent, Leonard: I feel as safe as a house.'

'Keep it, Revs, keep it. We'll look after that later. In the meantime what news? You've got to get Davy off the set.'

'He's come off, about five minutes ago. Collapsed. I've got him on the floor wrapped up in an Irvin jacket. It's the best I can do.'

'Good for you, Revs. I'm glad we've got you to look after him. Can he speak, or understand what's being said to him?'

'Yes, on and off.'

'Well, tell him we know where we are and that we don't need W/T.'

'Yes, I will, he's worrying about that. Do you know we're short of a parachute? Desmond wanted to keep it dark, but I guess you can take it.'

'What happened to it?'

'Burnt to bits.'

'I see. Have you fixed Davy up in case the aircraft falls apart?'

'Yes, we've tied a long string to the rip-cord of a 'chute. Then all we have to do is throw him out and hang on to the string.'

'Good, Revs, good.'

'Shall I go back to the turret? It's as clear as daylight, and above these white clouds we must stand out for miles.'

'I know, I've thought of that. No, stay where you are; if the fighters find us, they find us, that's all.'

'Can't you get into the clouds?'

'No, they're cumulonimbus: they'll be as bumpy as hell and I don't dare risk it.'

Davy called out for Revs, and Revs went back. There he stayed, sitting on the floor, both his arms round Davy, supporting him. Desmond was beside me, watching closely. He looked half asleep, but I knew that was not so: that he was on his toes, ready for whatever might happen. Taffy was in his seat, behind Desmond, looking out of the window for fighters, and idly twiddling his C.S.C. The minutes went by, and the moon fell gracefully lower, but the fighter attack we were waiting for never came. Below, the clouds were still as fleecy and dense as ever, inexorable as the moon. The secret we wanted so badly they refused to yield.

'I wonder if we're out to sea yet. It seems hours since we dropped the bombs. How long is it actually?'

'I don't know: about an hour and a half, I think.'

'Well, it's quarter past four: what time did we set course?'

'I can't remember: I've been trying to work it out.'

'Nor can I. I've no idea.'

But half an hour later came a break in the clouds and with it the yielding up of the secret. Land. Taffy said, 'Bloody hell!' and we went on in silence. At half past five we saw the sea, but it should have been England, if my calculations were right. Taffy bounced up and down in his seat and Desmond kicked him on the shin.

But after an hour all trace of the first wild jubilation was gone. While we were over land we still had parachutes, some of us, but over the sea they would not be much help. If we had known where we were, we would not have minded, but we did not know. At ten to seven we saw England, and that was only half the story. Cromer: the very same flashing light we had passed on the way out. Desmond and I looked at each other, and as before roared with laughter. For the first time since we had flown together our landfall was really and absolutely perfect.

'Revs, tell Davy I'm landing at the first aerodrome we see. God knows how he has stuck it.'

'He says to go on to Base: he wants to shoot a line to his friends.'

At five to eight I switched the engines off in front of the control tower, and an ambulance rushed Davy to hospital.

'Now talk, Revs.'

'I don't know much about it: I was too late for most of the action.'

'Quite, Revs. Now skip all that and give.'

'Yes, but it's true. The explosion knocked me out, and when I came round the moon was between my feet. Everything seemed dead quiet except for the rush of air, and I was convinced that the turret had been blown off and was crashing down on its own. All I can remember is thinking, "I hope to God it's over quickly", and saying, "I've been hit. I've been hit."'

'So it was you. No wonder I couldn't work it out.'

'I think I must have said it while I was still unconscious. I have only a vague memory of it. Then, for no reason whatsoever, I switched the light on, and to my absolute amazement it worked. I couldn't understand it, so I moved the turret control, and that worked too. It beat me altogether. In fact I imagined I was dreaming, and would probably have gone on sitting there for ever if I hadn't heard someone shout that the petrol tank was on fire, and then you saying, "Put it out, then." Sounded as if you wanted him to pass the butter, and I went off to see what I could do. What I saw when I got down there made my eyes pop out of my head. There wasn't any fuselage left on the port side at all, just an enormous gaping hole, and all along the floor up to the tank was a mass of flames and smoke. Desmond suddenly came up to me and told me to go back for my parachute, as he thought the tail might drop off at any moment. I didn't waste any time. By the time I'd got back the fire was almost out, but the incendiaries and the flares were smouldering, not to mention the spare ammunition. Taffy and Desmond were working like madmen throwing them overboard. We got most of them out, but those right on the port we couldn't get at for fear of falling out ourselves. The aeroplane seemed to be rolling about quite a bit: in fact, it's amazing to me that someone didn't fall out as it was. In the end I wedged myself round the flare-chute and hung on to Desmond's feet while he undid the straps. And so we got everything out. When we got back into the cabin Davy was on fire from top to bottom, with Taffy beating out the flames for all he was worth. The rest you know. Desmond went back for the first-aid kit, which was more than I should have liked to have done. Walking down the fuselage scared the life out of me.'

'Yes, Desmond was just as I expected he would be, only better.'

'I should like to know what went on down the fuselage before I got there. There was hell let loose when I arrived, and it had been going on for a long time before that. The flames were two feet high, and the air was so thick with smoke and cordite you couldn't see a thing. But Desmond and Taffy won't talk, and I don't suppose Davy remembers, even if he could speak.

'You know that both Taffy and Desmond deliberately crawled under the tank right into the middle of it and never stopped to think they were leaving their parachutes the wrong side. When I looked round and saw what was happening I thought it was only a matter of seconds before the tank would blow up. Nothing on earth would have induced me to do what they did. And still they won't talk.'

'Have you figured out what caused it all?'

'Yes, I've had the report from the armament experts. I know exactly what happened, now that you've come across. There were two shells. The first one, probably a 4·7, came through the front turret and exploded a few feet above us – not more than ten or twenty, the blast knocked me out flat. Taffy says there was a crash which lifted him off his stomach a fraction of a second before the explosion, so it's obvious the damage to the front turret was caused by the shell itself. Just as well it wasn't a contact fuse. All the hydraulics burst and Taffy's face was covered in oil. That's what I thought was blood when I first saw him standing in the well. He thought it was blood, too, and he says that from the expression in my eyes when I looked at him he believed he was dying. Well, I certainly thought he was going to die, and I never have been able to conceal my thoughts, so I don't blame him. The second shell must have burst almost simultaneously and behind the port wing. A piece of shrapnel from it hit one of the special flares in the rack and exploded it. They've found both the splinter and the fuse. The flare is worth several million candle-power and the flash lasts only a fraction of a second, so it's no wonder the port side of the fuselage came adrift. Davy at the time must have been kneeling over the flare-chute, only two feet away, and his head must have been turned to the starboard, or he would not have any face left at all. There remains the mystery of the second flare. It was in the chute, we know, because Davy had said he was standing by to drop it long before we started our run-up, and anyway the pin is still on the end of the wire; so someone must have pushed it out. Taffy and Desmond are positive it wasn't either of them, and it wasn't you, so it must have been Davy. He was totally blinded by the flash, and was obviously knocked silly – Desmond found him rolling about on his hands and knees shouting something about putting a fire out and not knowing in the least where he was: he only just grabbed hold of him in time to save him falling overboard. So God knows how he managed to push the thing out. You realize the chute is burnt to hell, and if that flare had been there there wouldn't have been any aeroplane left at all. It couldn't have helped exploding: Desmond could never have reached it in time, even if he had known anything about its existence.'

'Doc says he thinks he can save Davy's eyesight.'

'I know, he doesn't look it, but he's tough, and he's only eighteen.'

'He never complained once on the way home, and those burns must have been agony with all the cold wind. All he did was to talk about the wireless and from time to time ask how much longer before we landed. The only thing was he couldn't stand being left alone.'

'I'm going into town after lunch to see if I can say how-d'you-do to him. I don't suppose they'll let me in, but anyway, I don't feel like going to bed. After that I shall watch Fred Astaire in *Broadway Melody* with Penny, and then we're going on to a dance as a guest of the Wing Commander to celebrate Penny's engagement.'

'Penny engaged? He's only eighteen.'

'So's Davy, but then those eighteen-year-olds are a remarkable breed of men.'

Leave. The first of the year, and therefore the best. I met Maxine at the 'Mayfair'.

Her red hair sparkled, her mauve eyes glistened, and her quick smile was quicker than ever. We drank, and then we danced, and then we drank some more. Alf, behind the bar, was at his best: the blitz was at its height: London was exciting, yet somehow it was not excitement that I wanted; anyway, Maxine was to be married. I packed my bags and went home to Oxford. Oxford, in spite of its throngs of wealthy evacuees and silken-haired playboys, was peaceful and quiet.

I changed into grey flannels and an open shirt and wandered slowly through the streets, my hands in my pockets. An old lady stopped me and said:

'Is there anything the matter with you, my boy?'

'Yes,' I said. 'I've a broken heart.'

'Well, I never! That's no reason for an able-bodied young man like you not to be in uniform.'

And so, thinking of nothing to say, I passed along.

When I reported back from leave I found that many things had happened. Davy had regained his eyesight and after two serious relapses was on his way to recovery. The day I left Penny was shot down near Berlin, and with him Radley, our first wireless operator. The Wing Commander was missing too, with no hope of being saved. It seemed only yesterday that we had celebrated Penny's engagement.

CHAPTER SEVEN

WINTER

Then came winter, and with it my brother, Christopher. Christopher is younger than I, two years almost to the day. When war broke out he was in the middle of his second year at Oxford, studying law and, I think, liking it. He gave that up and joined the Air Force, and then, after a year of waiting around and training, he arrived up here in Yorkshire, only a few miles away and also on Whitleys. He is tall and blonde, with a youthful, sparkling laugh, and since we had not met for a year it was good to see him.

Winter, when she came, came unheralded and in force. First of all rain and mud. France and Belgium and Germany were steeped in snow, Yorkshire in mud. No matter where you went or what you did, there was mud. Mother sent me a pair of vast rubber-soled boots lined with sheepskin, and so life was a little easier. If we had operated from the aerodrome itself it would not have been so bad, but that was not to be. Our aeroplanes were kept five miles away in an advanced landing-field. True enough the field ran alongside a road, but it transpired that a vehicle capable of dealing with the mud around the gates had yet to be designed, and past the gates, where the mud became slightly less deep, the only available accommodation was a derelict farmhouse devoid of heating and infested by rats. On the nights that we operated we dressed up in the hangars ready for forty degrees of frost and piled into the bus, sweating and panting. From where the bus left us we had to walk, carrying our equipment in the dark and through the mud, sometimes as much as half a mile. Not far really, but we had been brought up to a life of ease and sitting down. The only legitimate complaint was that the mud and the water soaked our clothes, so that when we climbed into low temperature everything froze solid.

The mud lasted four weeks, and then, as the cold began to harden the ground, we were moved up further north. In those four weeks the results we achieved were small and the bombs we dropped were few, and for that matter far between. The weather was unkind, and that in more senses than one. Day after day the forecasts were doubtful, and in consequence day after day we stood by until the very last moment. The procedure was stereotyped. At dusk we dolled ourselves up, clambered into buses, and from them found our way into the aircraft. Then we settled ourselves in, 'ran up' and tested the engines, switched off, and stood by waiting for the order to take off or break it up, and more often than not we broke it up. It was a long, wearisome business; by the time we were back at the hangars it was too late to go out anywhere.

Of the crew, Taffy was the only one left. Desmond had a crew of his own, Revs was away on a course, and Stokey was sent on rest to a training-school. The loss took much of the joy of flying away; and I don't think we ever recaptured the same carefree teamwork. Of the trips themselves there was nothing much to recount, nothing other than routine. Sometimes we found the target, sometimes we did not. Sometimes the ack-ack was close and left its traces, but for the most part it was inaccurate and harmless. Curiously enough, it seemed always to be bursting away to starboard: for height and distance perfect, and obviously aimed at us, but none the less always to starboard. On the third consecutive time that this happened I looked at Taffy and could not help but laugh.

'You think we're over there, you b—s, don't you? Well, we're bloody well not.'

Taffy's face, when I looked at him working away or peacefully sleeping, reminded me of old times and always made me smile, but for the most part the laughter was gone. The excitement, such as there was, came mostly from the ground. The German took to his former habit of strafing us, generally speaking at dawn and dusk. The dawn part was no worry: I remained sound asleep. But his evening appearances were apt to be disconcerting. He came right down, below the level of the hangars, so that the bullets of the ground defence guns were as great a danger as those from the skies. One night – I was not flying, but helping the flarepath party – a German appeared overhead just as Dave of 'A' flight was taking off. It was too late; no one could warn him, and accidentally he was burning his navigation lights. The German pilot was bold and skilful; he opened his first attack at 800 feet, coming in from dead astern and setting the port engine on fire. There was no answering burst from the Whitley's rear gunner, so either his guns were not cocked or else he was put out of action too soon. As the flames began to spread and Dave lost height in an effort to regain the flarepath, the German delivered a second attack, and this time kept close in behind, firing all the time at point-blank range, right up to the moment the Whitley hit the deck. The ground defences were unable to open up because both aircraft were too close together. Out of the wreckage, three were still alive because of Dave's action in dragging them clear, but next day Dave was the only one left, and he was badly burned.

Up north, at our new station, came the cold: and as usual I was caught unprepared. I hate flying high: I hate the trouble of climbing: I hate having to use oxygen – the mask scratches my face: I hate not being able to see the ground, and I hate the violent change in temperature, so I have never flown above 8,000 feet, except once to clear the Alps. At 8,000 feet I know how cold it is likely to be, and so I put on just enough clothing, because I hate sweating about on the ground overladen with clothes. But, as I say, I was caught unprepared. The target was Mannheim; the weather was very bad: just as they forecast – snowstorms and frosts and lightning.

Very soon after take-off we lost the air-speed indicator, the electric heater burned out, and in a few minutes the pitot-head was frozen solid. We were in thick cloud and without a horizon; I found it difficult to judge what speed we should be flying at. We staggered along for many, many minutes, climbing very slowly, until eventually we broke cloud, and then I saw that the reason for our slow climb was that I had the nose far too high and therefore I had too low an air speed. The break lasted long enough for me to mark off mentally on the gyro in what attitude we should be flying, and then the clouds closed in again. The ice that had formed on the wings and superstructure was still with us, and as the minutes slipped by it became slowly thicker.

There seemed no end to the clouds: 'met' were certainly right. Lightning and bumps with a vengeance; it was difficult to keep the aircraft steady enough for Taffy to write up his log. Martin, the second pilot, was not yet happy enough at night-flying, so he stayed in the front turret. Slowly and painfully we climbed higher and higher in an effort to get above the clouds. The controls began to go solid and the air grew colder every minute. At 11,000 feet there were 58° of frost: the wings were coated with a layer of clear glaze, and inside the cabin it looked as though it had been snowing. At 13,000 ice began to form everywhere inside, and the outside of the perspex was covered with thick crystal rime. Surely it could not last much longer: my feet and hands were petrified, and we had to pull Martin out of the turret and lay him on the floor, because the whole of his body was covered by a thick coating of snow.

The noise of the ice flying off the props and beating against the fuselage was beginning to get on my nerves. At 15,500 we appeared to be clear of cloud, but the gauge showed 69° of frost and Taffy's navigation table was hidden in a solid inch of ice so that he could not even get at his maps. This appeared to amuse him, because all he did was to say 'Cheese' at regular intervals and fix the whole doings with a fascinated stare. I once read about somebody who was so cold that he set about beating his head on the floor to relieve the pain. I laughed at the time, but I think I understand now. Our E.T.A. was very rough, since the air speed had been purely guesswork, but we worked it out as best we could and started to lose height.

As soon as we came into cloud again the icing started afresh, but at least it grew warmer. I unplugged my intercom because the crackle of static on the aerial seemed to be bursting my eardrums. At 10,000 feet the starboard motor stopped: I put her into rich mixture and she picked up for a moment but then spluttered and finally petered out. The perspex was completely frosted over and we could not open any of the windows. At 7,000 feet the port motor began to cough and backfire. Taffy reported we were out of cloud, at least he thought we were, but that it was snowing heavily and there was no chance of seeing the ground. When, at 5,000 feet, both engines were running smoothly again, we thanked God for small mercies and set course for home.

It was a temptation to drop the bombs while we were still over Germany and so rid ourselves of the extra weight, but we restrained ourselves, because we knew the Channel ports were clear. We stayed below cloud all the way back and no one even bothered to fire at us – maybe they thought no more of the snow and sleet than we did. At the Belgian coast our landfall was 70 miles out and 40 minutes later than we expected, but at least we dropped some bombs on Boulogne. Somehow it seemed a roundabout way of going about things, and at interrogation none of us had much to say for ourselves. No more, for that matter, did the station commander.

The next trip we made was to Berlin. Once again 'met' reported severe icing conditions reaching up to 15,000 or 16,000 feet. This time I adopted different tactics. I put my faith in the forecast and flew all the way below it, at 1,000 feet. Unfortunately we passed clear over Den Helder, where the guns were unusually active, but they missed us. The clouds broke, but not before we had begun to think we were going to look stupid; none the less they did break and we climbed up to our height without so much as hearing the rattle of ice off the airscrews. The others were not so fortunate: they tried a straight climb and ran into more than they had bargained for. In fact all of them except Jackie were forced to turn back. Jimmy suffered the most. He lost both engines fifty miles out to sea and was down to 2,000 feet before they picked up again: what was more, he nearly lost his nose through frost-bite. Poor old Jimmy.

Then came Christmas. Festivities were somewhat curtailed, as we stood by until late the previous evening waiting to know whether we were to operate or not, and the mess was almost deserted, but we did our best. Taffy and I, with support from nearly all the flying crews, tried to call on some of the prison camps and drop food and Christmas wishes, but permission was refused: instead we celebrated ourselves. Lofty was back: good for Lofty. Four months he had been away at training-school, and they had been unable to hold him any longer. So, as he had always done, he did what he wanted, and came back to the Squadron. We ordered champagne and kissed the W.A.A.F.s under the mistletoe – in Jimmy's case under the disapproving eye of the station commander as well – and in general made a nuisance of ourselves as best we knew how. Before lunch we drank a toast to the future and reunion. There were seven of us in all: Lofty, Desmond, Jimmy, Frammy, Lousy and Lib and myself. Lib was new – we called him Doc, because before the war he was studying medicine – but the others, Frammy and Lousy, were older members of the Squadron than I was. In all it was a happy party. Lofty was now a newly-wed, and never have I seen him look better or more cheerful.

Desmond was lamenting Pluto, his faithful and all but human bloodhound, which had been shot by a local farmer. Jimmy was much the same as ever, full of brawn and muscle and oozing beer after twelve days' leave– he had been in bed for forty-eight hours recovering – the others were free from care and making the most of a good opportunity for a party. If nothing else, we had good reason for celebrating. Eight nights ago the most successful raid ever – Mannheim, a reprisal for Coventry. When we set course for home there were twenty-six fires raging and we were only the middle formation of the attack. We went there again two nights later, and some of the fires were still burning.

Taffy, in the front turret, had behaved like a small boy coming unexpectedly face to face with Father Christmas, and kept shouting a mixture of 'wizard' and 'cheese' down the intercom.

The festivities lasted two days and then we went back to work. Christopher did his first trip, to Bremen, and enjoyed it in spite of the cold. Revs came back, primed with knowledge about fighters and guns. Desmond had started off with a bang and was forging ahead. One day early in January take-off was at half past four, in broad daylight. I was not flying and so went down to the hangars to watch. The air was cold, but dry and very clear. Tommy, Desmond's sturdy wireless op., was coming out of the Crew Room.

'How are you doing, Tommy?'

'Fine, sir.'

'What's the hurry?'

'I've lost my mascot.'

'Mascot?'

'Yes, my little fluffy black dog. Do you remember?'

'Why, of course I remember. Taffy kept it on the navigation table all the time and wouldn't stop stroking it. Yes, I remember it.'

'I've never ever in my life flown without it, not even on a local air test, and now I can't find it. I haven't seen it since the trip I did with you to Merigniac.'

I mustered four airmen and sent them to help look, but we never found it. Desmond came up.

'Have you seen Taffy, Leonard?'

'No, I haven't.'

'He's leaving today, isn't he?'

'No, tomorrow morning, to night fighters.'

'I've got fifty Players for him. Mother sent me a box of fifty for each of the crew: they're in my locker. Would you see he gets them?'

'Yes, I will.'

'Things haven't been the same since we split up: I feel sad. Get hold of Taffy's address, won't you? I couldn't stand it if we lost touch.'

'I know; don't rub it in.'

'I must go. I've got a note here. If I shouldn't come back, will you send it to, you know who?'

'No. I mean yes. You know what I mean. How do you feel about tonight?'

'Fine, it should be a good trip.'

But there was something in his eyes I had not seen before.

'Give yourself plenty of height, and whatever you do keep a good lookout for fighters: they've taken to patrolling just off the coast these last few days.'

And so Desmond hopped into the back of the van and

disappeared, with a grin on his face and his thumbs in the air. He had trouble starting up and took off quarter of an hour after the others.

I walked back to the mess with Gaudie, the Adjutant. As we came round the side of the hangar we saw something which pulled us up short.

'God, man, look at that! Have you ever seen anything so beautiful in your life? If it weren't for the cold I'd sit down and paint it right here.'

Flaming red. I have never seen the sky so flaming red: great angry streaks sweeping away from the horizon and a background of orange and pale, frosty blue.

'Yes, it's beautiful all right, but it's a beauty I could do without just now. You don't usually get skies like that for nothing.' Desmond flew out of the largest red streak, dipped his wings right overhead and set course, out towards Hamburg. Gaudie and I went in to tea.

An hour later a message came in from Jimmy saying that he was returning through engine failure. At eight-fifteen they were due off the target. I went along to Control to see what news there was. Rix had lost an engine over the enemy coast and was coming back: a bad night. Jackie and Frammy had sent 'Mission completed' and were on their way back home. A bit early yet. Jimmy walked in, looking somewhat crestfallen for once and very hot – more than I was. He said something had happened 50 or 60 miles off the coast. A large ball of fire had appeared just behind him, and after hanging in the sky for a while it had dropped into the sea. He had circled the area for a while, but failed to pick anything out. An hour and a half later I came back. Frammy, Lousy and Lofty were well on their way home: five others had sent 'Mission completed', Rix was just about due: but no news from Desmond.

The air-raid siren wailed. Jimmy and I went outside. An aircraft was approaching from the east. Over to the west, a long way off, there was a barrage of A.A., probably Liverpool or Merseyside. The aircraft came overhead and started to circle. It was a Whitley – Rix. He came through on R/T asking permission to land. One engine was dead: the other was running well: he still had his bombs with him. Control told him there were hostile raiders in the vicinity and to come in quickly. The barrage over Liverpool increased in intensity. Rix finished circling and throttled back. The tempo of his engines quickened as he put the exactors into fine pitch. Then, as he crossed the boundary marker, dead silence. He was holding off.

'Good, he's made it.'

'He'll be sent on rest now. Deserves it too.'

An awful, rending crash and suddenly dead silence.

'That's the end of Rix.'

And Jimmy and I ran for our lives. On the aerodrome there was confused shouting and the sweep of headlights. Somewhere in the middle was a dark, shapeless mass: in the dark it was impossible to make out anyone or anything.

'Put those lights out, you bloody fools: there's a German overhead. Can't you hear him? And hurry with those extinguishers.'

I bumped into someone. It was Rix. 'Good God, man, I thought you were dead.'

'Thanks. No, I'm all right.'

'What happened?'

'There's an obstruction just by the boundary.'

'That's no obstruction. It's "N". My "N". The "N". They brought it back today after putting a new fuselage on it.'

'Well, it's "N" no more. I hit it. I came in low on purpose because I knew we wouldn't be able to round again on one engine. I must have misjudged it a little.'

I flung myself flat, and a stick of bombs exploded somewhere in the direction of the hangars. The commotion died down, the armourers arrived to debomb the crash and we went back to Control. On the table were plotted the homecoming aircraft. All of them were more or less in a bunch and more or less on track. They would be overhead in half an hour: Frammy first. But no sign of Desmond.

Revs walked in, and shortly afterwards Frammy landed. Control was busy. Four aircraft were circling already: the clouds were closing in, and there were hostile raiders in the neighbourhood. All lights were extinguished except the flare-path, and that was visible only from 1,000 feet. Landings had to be controlled, and no time was lost. There were other air-craft from other squadrons operating as well, and 'phone calls kept coming through, asking for news of so-and-so, who might be lost or had failed to maintain communication. In all it was a busy evening: Revs and I were the only watchers.

'"P" for Peter up on R/T, wants to know if he can come in and land: he's having trouble with his port motor.'

'Who is it?'

'Lofty.'

'He's O.K. Tell him to wait till "R"'s down. He's making his approach now: another five minutes, that's all.'

'O.K.'

'"Q" for Queenie's come up on D.F. 326 – he's away south of track. Strength 7 – he should be here in twenty minutes.'

'Good, that's the last one, isn't it?'

'No, "M" for Mother's outstanding. Haven't heard a sound from them since take-off.'

'"M" for Mother: who's that?'

'Desmond.'

'Who's his wireless operator?'

'Tommy; he's good. You can rule out any possibility of him not coping with the set, unless it's been hit, of course, which is always a possibility.'

'Maybe he's been working another station.'

'No, I've tried that. Group has no trace of him at all.'

'"R"'s down O.K.'

'What about the Observer Corps? Have they any plots?'

'They say there's an aircraft believed to be a Whitley circling the Newcastle district, and another one down near Doncaster flying north-west, above cloud.'

'They're both a long way off track, but you never know. Ring up Group and find out what aircraft from other squadrons are outstanding.'

'They're all down except five, and two of those are homing at the moment.'

'Sounds more hopeful. Keep in touch with the Observer Corps. I'll have D.F. call Desmond again.'

Slowly the minutes went by. Frammy, Lousy and Lofty

came in. They reported good visibility over the target but intense anti-aircraft fire. Somebody gave me a cup of tea, and Lofty stayed behind.

'There's a Whitley landed in Acklington.'

'Who is it?'

'I don't know. They're going to ring us back.'

'I hope to hell they hurry; he's fifty minutes overdue already.'

'What about the other one?'

'Still heading north-west; somewhere in the Leeds district, I think.'

Once more we sat and waited. The 'All Clear' sounded; away in the distance the Liverpool barrage had died down. Revs grew restless and began pacing the room. The Lorenz indicator, with its array of indicators and green lights, kept clicking over regularly, once every second. For a while it was the only sound to be heard. I lit another cigarette and noticed my forefinger was stained with nicotine. A telephone rang. I started up and then sat down again. The crew at Acklington were not Desmond's.

'That leaves only two unaccounted for.'

'Ring up the Observer Corps again.'

Another hour went by.

'Five to four: a maximum of ten minutes' petrol left.'

'I've checked on the Observer Corps. Every single aircraft that has crossed the coast tonight has been accounted for, except this one circling the Leeds area. It's still above cloud and no one has been able to contact it. Apparently there's no sign of anything coming in from the sea.'

'That still leaves two adrift altogether, then, does it?'

'Yes.'

'I wish to Christ they'd stop that bloody indicator thing clicking. I've done nothing but listen to it now for four hours.'

'Hold it, Revs, hold it. It may be the only thing that Desmond's got to bring him in.'

The buzzer on the Group telephone line buzzed.

'The Observer Corps aircraft crashed twenty miles north of Leeds.'

'Crashed?'

'Yes.'

'What about the crew?'

'Nothing known. Ring you back later.'

'Quarter past four. No matter what he did or he didn't do, Desmond must be down now, one way or the other.'

Twenty minutes later the Group buzzer buzzed for the last time. The aircraft that crashed near Leeds was a Wellington, not a Whitley.

Lofty's eyes looked down at me from out of his long black stubble, and he said:

'It's always the worthwhile people who go; the scum, like you and me, stay on for ever.'

'I know, Lofty, don't rub it in.'

Three weeks later Lofty himself went missing. Lofty, the one person in the Squadron I thought would never go.

CHAPTER EIGHT

HALIFAXES

With that I was posted away from Whitleys to another squadron, equipped with four-engined Halifaxes. The aircraft were new, and as yet not ready to operate; in consequence there followed a period of training and development. Whitleys had been homely and simple, but here was a new atmosphere altogether: new equipment, new technique of flying and everything vastly more complicated. And so, as I had done once before, I threw myself into hibernation – to learn.

Throughout the hours of this long hibernation there was time in abundance to meditate, and nothing but memories to live on. The memories were sweet and often exhilarating. The carefree, cheerful life: the trust and companionship in danger: the splendour of success: the frustration of failure. These were the quantities that made the memories sweet, but behind all this there was an unescapable note of sadness. When Napoleon considered the appointment of a new general, he invariably asked: 'Is he lucky?' Time and again I have wondered at that, but now I know that Napoleon was right. A.A. defences fire a barrage which is either predicted on an individual aircraft or which is wholly indiscriminate and merely covers a particular objective. If it is indiscriminate the issue naturally is one of luck and luck only. If it is predicted, the matter resolves itself into a contest of skill with the odds slightly in favour of the aircraft. The barrage may take many various forms, and for each of them there is a different counter tactic. Consequently the ace pilot, provided he never makes a single mistake, should be able to forestall every barrage he ever meets. If he is an ace, he knows what the guns are going to do next, and therefore he can outwit them: he just won't be where they expect him to be when the shells explode. But – and this is the point – assuming he can do all this, the net result is merely that he has resolved the issue to a matter of luck pure and simple. Very few shells go exactly where they are meant to: if for that reason alone, there is always this basic element of luck. A bad pilot can fly straight and level through the heaviest barrage in the world and come out with not so much as a scratch: a first-class pilot may fly straight into a shell that through faulty manufacture exploded 5,000 feet lower than it ought to have done. There is nothing that anyone can do about it, and because of it many of the finest captains in the world have gone missing.

Lofty, to my knowledge, never made a mistake, yet he was shot down. Desmond never made a mistake either. He collided with an incoming German bomber over the North Sea. He could not even have seen it. It speaks for itself. I thought of the many times that through sheer stupidity and carelessness I had literally asked to be shot down, and the knowledge brought a sense of sadness. A struggle for existence in which the strongest survives is something I can well understand; in fact it is what I have always believed to be the essence of life. What I cannot understand is a struggle for existence in which survival hinges on luck. Yet there must be an explanation, and so it is that I say our values must be all upside-down and that a long life does not really count for much in the long run. It isn't much comfort, though, is it? I suppose that is the point.

Occasionally news filtered through of the others. Christopher was going strong: had completed five trips and was due for a crew of his own. I saw him from time to time, once or twice for tea, but mostly in the evenings. He seemed to be his same smiling self: still flaxen hair and a young, fresh-coloured face. As usual, the girls, and not he, seemed to be doing most of the chasing. His only worry was his sergeant-captain, who, in the course of two trips, had succeeded in spinning accidentally out of a cloud and in flying defiantly through a hedge in mistake for the flarepath. There was other news too: among it that Lib was missing with little hope of being alive, and that Frammy had crashed and killed himself. Davy had come back to the Squadron and had started operating once more. Incredible but true. Then one day there happened a miracle: Taffy walked into the Crew Room and said he had come to join me. Good old Taffy: we fell into each other's arms, to the evident astonishment of the other sergeants, and laughed into each other's eyes, and then we went to work.

Stokey was still at training-school, hating it, and likely to be there for some time. He asked to be allowed to join us; we tried too, but permission was not granted. There remained Revs, but there again permission was not granted. We shrugged our shoulders and collected ourselves a new crew. Second pilot – tough, bronzed Jerry, with the experience of ten Whitley trips behind him. Wireless operator – Jacko: five foot eleven, twelve stone; had boxed and played football for the R.A.F.; knew no fear and could not find anything he did not know of the wireless set. Engineer – Brown; boasted many years' experience in the Merchant Navy and an extraordinary adaptability no matter what the difficulty. Second wireless op – Gutteridge; light brown hair, a fair moustache and a girl friend – about to be fiancée – in town. Rear gunner – unknown. We settled down to get to know each other and in the course of two months' work and jollification, continually in each other's company, we emerged a team, as we thought, to be proud of.

Then came news of Revs. At first it was more or less a rumour, but before long we heard the full story. A few nights ago he was flying with his Flight Commander: the weather was truly appalling, and over the target they were hit by an A.A. shell which put the compass out of action. The wind was very strong, about eighty miles an hour as it turned out, and the clouds were dense. Consequently they had little with which to navigate. After two and a half hours of worry and strain they saw the coast, more or less on E.T.A. Whereabouts it was they did not know, but before them was an aerodrome, lit up and in action. They circled it and decided to come in: the flarepath gave them a green, and they made their approach. The night was very dark, so they could see nothing but the flarepath lights, but Revs thought they looked somehow strange and unfamiliar. As they were holding off, only a few feet from the ground, the aerodrome control pilot gave them a red. They were already near the end of the flarepath, but by the skin of their teeth they cleared the boundary obstructions. At 700 feet, as they were coming round for the second approach, they looked down and saw that the aerodrome was on an island. There are no islands off the East Coast of England: it was Holland.

An hour and five minutes later, amid violent bumps and down-currents, they ran out of petrol. The wireless was out of action: they did not know where they were, nor did anyone else. They thought they were over sea; anyway, they gambled on that, and did not jump. Revs dashed out of his turret and collected the crew in the fuselage, ready to alight on the water. There was not much time; time enough to free the dinghy and brace themselves against the shock of hitting the sea: nothing else. The touch-down, as it happened, was as light as a feather, but almost immediately a mass of water swept through the door and the lights went out. In the sudden black-out they were hopelessly blinded and because of the waves they could hardly stand. Revs waded through to the dinghy and somehow managed to throw it out, but the cord snapped and the swell flung the dinghy out of sight. Revs wasted no time: dived out after it and scrambled on. The others followed him quickly, like rats out of a hole. Revs hauled Martin and Alf aboard in rapid succession and at the same time grabbed hold of Bill's hand. Bill could not swim a stroke: was drowning and asking for help. Martin passed out, face down in the dinghy and was useless from then on. Alf was face down too, but he was still conscious. The waves were gigantic, about ninety feet high, and the wind made a roar like the rending of linen. Bill's weight was too great to hold for long; each wave, as it came along, passed over the dinghy and drenched them all to the skin. Revs beat on Martin's head with all his strength to wake him up, and shrieked to Alf for help. Alf said: 'I can't, you're kneeling on me,' and Revs realized suddenly that it was the truth. He moved, and Alf caught Bill's other hand. Between them, and after the very greatest difficulties, they dragged him on board. And that was not the end: he fell face down into the flooded dinghy and there was not room to pull him and Martin upright without falling out themselves. When at last everybody was righted, the aircraft was a long way behind them. They each knew what had been in the other's mind, and that was why not a word had been said; but it was better to save a man they already had hold of than to forsake him and go after a man they could not even see.

For a brief instant, as they were swept up on to the top of a wave, they had a fleeting vision of a Whitley silhouetted against the horizon, and, standing on its fuselage, their Flight Commander. And that was the end. Against the furied roar of the waves they drifted away towards the dawn. They did not know the Flight Commander's brother was not to return that night either.

The gale had been blowing for thirty-six hours and showed no signs of abating. The hope of being rescued was slight. It was midwinter; no one even knew they were in the sea, let alone their position: the dinghy was full of water, and in one place was torn. They plugged the hole with a handkerchief and used a cap to bale, but they needed all the energy they had to remain inside the dinghy, and baling was very difficult. Two hours later dawn broke. The navigator began beating his legs to bring them back to life and discovered the legs belonged to the rear gunner. One of the crew asked the time.

When he heard it was only five past nine he pulled out a clasp-knife and tried to cut his throat.

But Revs stayed his hand and said:

'No, you're not. If you want to do yourself in, go ahead and throw yourself overboard, but you're not going to do anything inside this dinghy.'

The man laughed, and for ever after remained sane. Two of them felt sea-sick, but forgot to do anything about it when they saw an aircraft flying towards them. They fired a Very cartridge, then another, and as the plane came overhead they saw it was a Heinkel 111. Two more hours went by, and another aircraft approached. It was a Blenheim, and it too came right overhead, but, try as they might, none of them was able to fire a cartridge. The pistol was loaded, Revs had his forefinger round the trigger, but that was as far as he could get, and the Blenheim disappeared from view.

As the hours went by and the fury of the waves continued unabated, a chilled silence slowly enveloped the dinghy. One by one each of the four men had bared his soul. One by one they had recounted the story of their lives; not the story that you or I recount to our sweethearts or in a sudden burst of confidence, but the story of their souls; the story of their petty hates and their jealousies and their prides: in other words, the one and only story in the world that they had thought would die with them, for ever untold. But now that this was over, now that each man had looked up to God and offered up, as it were, an apology for being human, there remained only memories, and silence. And with that apology went, as must be, the last vestige of hope. In its place the cold and the wet brought to each man something they had never known before, an overpowering, subconscious coma which left them careless of whether they were rescued or not.

It was a cold and sunny March morning that Revs walked into the mess. For his work in rescuing the crew that day on the sea he was given the choice of where to go, and he chose to come and join Taffy and me. He looked the same, lean and smiling, but his face showed that inside were locked for life three secrets, and his eyes bore the trace of eternal gratitude to the Navy. With him he brought news of the others. Jimmy had sailed for America to visit the U.S. Army Air Corps and fetch back an American-built bomber: Lousy had flown into a balloon barrage and was dead: the Wing Commander had been shot down in the sea but was safe in Germany. Christopher had been moved further north still, but I saw him from time to time. He had his own crew, and a crew at that to be proud of: and furthermore, in spite of his young years and his relatively small flying experience, he was already accepted as a crack pilot and captain. I looked into his blue eyes and saw that they glistened with excitement in a life which should have kept away a little longer but which was already part of him.

At last came the long-overdue news, the news we had all been praying for. Operations. Revs was not to come with us. No one could fathom why not, but none the less he was not to come. He was an R.A. – I had not known that until recently – and we made use of him to design us a mascot. It was a little late, but none the less he produced a masterpiece – a symbolic cat, holding Hitler's head between his front paws. As such it might sound funny to an outsider; but the cat was for a reason – and as he saw us into the aircraft the paint was still wet. The trip was commonplace. The weather was excellent, we saw the target – Kiel – and dropped all our bombs inside the area of the docks, starting two large fires. The ack-ack, to Taffy's disgust, was intense and left us with a few holes, and on the way home we were fired at by a fighter. Instead of Revs, we had in the tail Hares, small, vivacious and straight from training school. When he saw the opening burst he volunteered his first speech of the night, and then at the top of his voice:

'Come in, you b—: come in, you lousy, flat-faced b—! Come on: I'll give you what you're waiting for! I'll teach you to come messing around with Mr. C—'

Taffy started bouncing up and down in his seat, jerking his thumb, roaring with laughter and shouting alternately 'Cheese' and 'Wizard'. But the fighter never came, and we returned unmolested. The only unpleasant moment of the trip, as it happened, was the take-off. As we settled down in our seats the air raid warning sounded, and a few moments later the ground-defence guns went into action. Against the noise of the engines it was impossible to hear what was happening, and so many lights burning made us feel as conspicuous as a drunken sailor at a temperance meeting. As we took off some bombs fell harmlessly across the boundary of the 'drome, and when we landed back there was a forlorn German Wing Commander having bacon and eggs in the mess. He had not been shot down: his engines had failed.

This trip shut the lid on our three months' training and offered a vista of hope and excitement. Our step became jaunty and our appetites capacious, but three days later the Squadron was grounded pending the completion of various technical modifications, and the crews were disbanded. Of the pilots, two were to go to America for flying duties. We collected in the Adjutant's office to draw lots, and Willy, a burly New Zealander, and I won. Somewhat sadly, but none the less optimistically, I said farewell to Revs and Taffy and Jacko and Jerry and Guttridge and Brown and Hares, spent a happy evening with Christopher, and packed my bags.

CHAPTER NINE

AMERICAN ROMANCE

On a fine May morning we hoisted the anchor and sailed away. The trees and hedgerows were wreathed in blossom, the grass was green and the birds were singing. I stood up in the bows, my chest bared to the breeze, and revelled in the beauty and the change of atmosphere. Willy sidled up and said, 'Do you realize that at any moment from now on we are liable to hit a mine?' and I moved aft behind the shelter of the poop – at least the thing that I call the poop. Actually I had been under a misapprehension for twenty-four hours, because when we came on board I took it for granted that this was merely a ferry which was to take us out to the real boat. However, from what I could gather from the crew – they being all Norwegian – it was a good 900 tons, in other words quite a bit smaller than a cross-Channel packet, and provided the sea was not too rough there was a good chance of our getting across safely. Eventually we picked up the escort and the rest of the convoy and headed out into Mid-Atlantic. From then on followed a ding-dong battle amongst the convoy as to who was not going to occupy the flank position. Our skipper must have been pretty slick; he stayed firmly in the centre from start to finish.

Willy and I were the only Bomber Command personnel on board: the rest, six of them, were Coastal Command merchants, with very curious ideas. They were armed to the teeth with all the intricate paraphernalia of coastal navigation, and, after carefully preparing a so-called 'North Atlantic Chart' on a piece of scrap-paper, made a habit of breezing up to the Captain and telling him where he was. The Captain was a large and genial man, but he had been at sea for thirty-six years and consequently he was not at all favourably impressed. They also had a stock of technical terms such as Abaft, Aloft, Splicing the Mainbrace, Scuppers, Galley and countless others, which they used shamelessly on every conceivable occasion without so much as an attempt at explaining their meaning. Willy unexpectedly blossomed out into an orgy of reading, writing and washing his clothes, so that we practically never saw him, and I was left to withstand the brunt of the Coastal onslaught on my own.

They inveigled me into playing cards by saying that the last Bomber Command pilot on board had lost £23 10s. in a matter of a week, but nevertheless it passed the time of day, and at the end of the voyage, when I had won £20, they said it was too much and gave me £3 10s. Gradually, as I knew would happen, the sea grew rougher, until finally the only means of tasting fresh air was to put your head out of a window and hope not to be drowned in the process. The effect on Willy was remarkable; in fact, I almost believe he enjoyed it; he broke a three hours' silence by staggering to his feet and saying he was off to 'batten down the hatches'. It was obvious from the way he said it that he had devised some means of alleviating the agony – though quite what it was I could not for the life of me think – but unfortunately he was not very successful. As far as I was concerned, the only visible result was that we were deprived of all fresh air, and spent the rest of the day rolling about the room gasping for breath.

But this was by no means all. News came through that the *Hood* had been sunk and that the *Bismarck* was rapidly bearing down on us. Up to this moment it had just been possible to understand the gist of what the crew were saying, but from now on even that was done away with: the only hope was to watch their gestures closely and try thereby to glean some information. But even that did not always succeed, because they took to the habit of popping a head round the corner, dashing something off in Norwegian and then quickly disappearing. That night I was lying in bed – when I say 'lying' I mean, of course, trying not to fall out too often – listening to the crack of the keel as it hit the water and trying to drown Willy's peaceful snores, when the door burst open and in dashed Gibbs of Coastal Command, hidden beneath the folds of a Mae West and a life-saving jacket.

'What's bitten you? Found some gin on board or something?'

'Put your lifebelt on.'

'Don't be a bloody fool!'

'Put your lifebelt on – it's your only hope.'

'Beat it, Gibbs, beat it. I'm not in the mood.'

'They've just sunk a ship to forrard, and others have been torpedoed astern.'

'Where?'

'Astern.'

'Somebody's got darned good eyesight.'

Gibbs dashed out again. Willy grunted and said: 'If the bloody ship's going down, I'm bloody well going to die peacefully in bed.'

'So am I, Will boy.' And curiously enough I went to sleep.

Some days later we docked at a Canadian port. Willy and I reported to Canadian Pacific and found they knew not a thing about us – who we were or why we were there. After twenty-four hours they discovered our names on a list and said we would have to see Captain Snooks, but Captain Snooks was busy at a conference. We hung around in a sweltering passage for four hours, and then in desperation I brushed the secretary aside and marched into the office. Captain Snooks was reclining in a chair, his feet on the desk, smoking a cigar. I did my best to explain what I had come for.

'Can you fly?'

'Average. I've not broken an aeroplane to date.'

'Let's see your qualifications.'

'I've flown with the R.A.F.'

'Hours?'

'Seven hundred.'

'What about navigation? How many courses have you taken?'

'None. I haven't really had time the last eighteen months or so.'

'You'll have to start as a second pilot.'

'Second pilot?'

'That's what I said.'

'I've flown four-engined aircraft in England, and operated in them, if it comes to that.'

'I can't help what you've done in England. A mere 500 miles' flight to the Continent and back is a very different matter from flying the Atlantic.'

'Yes, I appreciate that.'

'You will leave your address here and await instructions. That is all.'

Willy got out of the room just in time, but only just, and he is normally one of the mildest men I have met. Then out of the storm came a brilliant ray of sunshine – Jimmy. Jimmy looking fitter and ruddier and better-fed than ever. And Percy was with him. If I had not had an excruciating stomach-ache I should have kissed them both on the spot. Instead we nattered inconsequentially until dusk and then, leaving our address, we caught the night south-bound express.

New York. A city full of secrets, and all of them new to me. For four days and four nights a riot. Cocktails, dances, drives through the city. Times Square on Broadway, Park Avenue, overhead railways, La Guardia airfield, people who take you as you come, not as they come. And no sleep. Life was too good to waste time sleeping anyway, but as it happened people had too much friendship to offer to let us sleep. Why, *God* alone knows. An American in England would never find the same hospitality, and he knows it only too well, but that seems to make no difference to him. Then, after it all, an invitation to spend a quiet evening! Dinner and cocktails in the warmth of a 62nd Street garden, and a mysterious hostess called Constance. But the evening, as it turned out, was not so quiet. Cocktails in the garden – yes. But the dinner at La Belle Meunière and afterwards dancing at Fifi's Monte Carlo. Drinks on the house, simply because we were Air Force pilots. A curious reason, but that's American. And then, because life was too good to waste time sleeping, a 5 a.m. drive out of New York.

Willy, Constance and I ranged in front; behind, amongst piles of luggage, a black Persian cat, two snow-white pigeons and a Scottie. We were a curious assortment, and out of the luxurious green Cadillac sprang a never-ceasing flow of dance music. Peace, empty roads, occasionally a cream-coloured police car and now and then a dead skunk: that was all. Losing the way amid rocks and green trees. Myself at the wheel, and the curious, unreal sensation of a left-hand drive. The quiet, light, thrilling surge of 84 horse-power. Gradually more and more cars and the sun hotter. Hot dogs at a pull-in because we felt hungry. And all three of us light-hearted, hysterical with laughing: our brains too weak to absorb anything but incoherent thoughts.

Then, after four hours' driving, Old Lyme in Connecticut. A white, wood-built house on a hill, a panorama of bright-green trees, reaching down to the haze of the sea; in the background, Long Island. Wild, scrub-like surroundings, evergreen grass, and a fluttering of butterflies. The scrunch of tyres on the drive and somewhere in the distance a sound of laughter. A coon, jet black against the spotless white of his coat, lounging happily in the sun of the verandah. For a while peace and rest: food under the shade of a tree, dark glasses, ice-cold highballs and orange-juice, and brains still half hysterical, only now a little quicker. A telephone bell, a warm Southern accent, and then more drinks, more journeys in the Cadillac. People standing on their doorsteps, beckoning us in. Sun and fathomless skies and the hum of mos-quitoes. Mother's exultant welcome; not my mother – Constance's mother. But in the warm and somehow vibrant atmosphere it seemed quite natural to call her mother, and so I did. I can't say why. Willy pushed his hands deeper in his pockets and started talking about peanut butter. Constance said, 'A woman is as old as she looks, and a man is old when he stops looking,' and our host hung a Union Jack over the porch.

Clams. Platefuls of them, salty and fresh from the sea, and Mother raised her glass: 'To the devil with that swine, and God bless England for boys like you two'; and Willy mum-bled something about New Zealand. Then, as the last stroke of midnight chimed out, the green Cadillac turned its nose towards home. The music was still there, alive and vibrant.

The warm night air was charged with some mysterious electricity, the stars shook themselves impatiently and shouted, 'Get on with it, get on with it: we're waiting,' and the crackling of the crickets broke suddenly through my brain. Once more the white wood-built house, and the scrunch of tyres on the drive. The music stopped, and in its place trickled the scurry of feet in the undergrowth – field mice? chipmunks? turtles? I didn't know. Down towards the sea, fireflies flickering through the trees, the eerie call of some unknown night bird, and behind us, boundless lights with no blackout. Some more music, home-made for a change, another highball, a black Persian cat prostrate on an unshuttered window-ledge, and Willy went to bed.

The days went by: the sun grew slowly hotter, and Willy and I stayed on with Constance.

New York, Old Lyme; Old Lyme, New York. A new world altogether, and the memory of war miles and miles away. Bathing, green trees, clams, breakfasts in the sun. A coal-black negro, quiet and ever in the background: mint juleps behind a Southern drawl. Dancing; sweltering streets; lights, skyscrapers; Sachs on Fifth Avenue; the Rainbow Room. Mother, ever vivacious and laughing, and forty years younger than her age; arguing with Constance for being never in time or too extravagant: 'God in heaven, woman, how many more summer dresses do you want? You don't need furs this time of year.' And praising the British as much as she loathed the Germans, until even Willy felt embarrassed. Constance, Willy and I staggering into yet another cocktail party, and everybody staring at us: 'Are you feeling ill?'

'Yes, Willy's suffering from sleepy-sickness: he's been to bed once or twice just lately.'

And Willy's frenzied snort: 'Christ, that man hasn't slept in his own bed for twelve nights!' And for the first time in his life he blushed, because it was not quite what he had meant to say.

A grand piano in 62nd Street.

'That's a beautiful piano, darling, and in point of fact no more so than the way you play it.'

'At least it has a history.'

'Meaning you've played on it too long?'

'George composed some of the "Rhapsody in Blue" on it.'

'George?'

'George Gershwin. After the show he used to come back here and strum on it. Mother got furious and kicked him out regularly every night at five to two. If it hadn't been for her I should have married him.'

'Good for Mother. I mean if you had, I shouldn't have met you. My music's not as good as what he composed for you, but I'll make up for it somehow else.'

Yes, but there's no end to this, and time is growing short. The memories are too many, and the remembrance too sweet. The magical electricity of the American atmosphere, the magical infection, too, of the men and women who live in it. Fireflies in a dark street, laughter in a troubled world, what's the difference? From Pat, the night watchman, to Deems Taylor of 'Fantasia' fame, they all seem genuinely pleased to see you.

People ask: 'What did you think of America?'

I answer: 'Here for the first time I have met real freedom, and that is all I am interested in.' There are other characteristics too: chiefly organization and competition. You get service, because if you do not like what you are getting you say, 'Right, I will go find it elsewhere,' and people know that you won't have far to go. And ever the background of unceasing friendliness and wit. But behind it all there was something else I detected, some indefinable undertone. At first I was puzzled: then I thought I understood. War. Here was a country seemingly at peace, but none the less a country preparing for war. Perhaps because of my perpetual state of coma, I saw a vista of limitless machinery, of wheels and cogs and pistons rolling into action, slowly but inexorably. And about their movement there was a devastating air of finality.

Once, when I had been arrested for an assortment of offences, I went along to the police station. They were very friendly and sympathetic and helpful, but all the time I knew that a machinery had been set in action which nothing I said or did could ever stop. It was the same thing here in New York: a mantle of pretence, and beneath it unceasing preparation. A curious sensation, like watching a play. At first, when everyone spoke shamelessly of wanting to fight against the Axis, I wondered why they did not stand up and do it. Then later I understood the answer. A nation 130 million strong, a population with vast foreign elements, a country 3,000 miles broad, and 48 different States. And, added to that, a continent 3,000 miles away from the theatre of war. England did not fight until she was directly affected – at least that is what I think – and equally America would not fight until she was directly affected, because even though 100 million of her subjects wanted to do so, nothing on earth could bring the remaining 30 into line. But all the same it would do your heart good to see the wartime welcome of these first 100 million citizens.

Then, as the days drew into July, we left Willy in Montreal and motored down South. Constance and myself. Omar the black Persian cat, and stifling heat. The sky was blue, the scenery was green, and on our right Lake Champlain was brown and cool and clear. We drove off the road among pine trees and parked the car. Omar slipped his lead and ran amok, so we caught him and locked him inside. The sun was very hot, and my limbs tingled from the freshness of the water. We lay down on the sand today and watched the children splashing in the lake. Nine days later we were married in a curious little church in Montreal. Jimmy was to have been one of the witnesses, but he left for home the same day. Instead we picked up a couple of strangers off the streets, and a good time was had by all. Two days later I was ordered back to England in a Hudson.

The heat, as usual, was stifling; it was good to get off the ground. We flew for six hours over scenery that because of its colouring and its novelty was exhilarating. The St. Lawrence looked lazy and contented: the green, billowing plains, specked with white-dotted villages, stretched mile after mile: the dull blue of the Gulf, unmarked by foam or sail, blinked up at us happily, and then came the barren waste of Newfoundland – a series of wooded, marshy tableaux, cracked by deep watery clefts. We landed at Newfoundland to refuel. The sun was at its height, and the dust ate through to the marrow in my bones, So we did not stop there long. As we sat in the plane waiting for the engines to warm up I turned in my seat and looked at the young faces of the navigator and the wireless operator. I thought: 'Two boys straight out of training-school with no experience of flying behind them, and twenty-four months ago I did not even know how to take off. If this was 1938 we would be making headline news, yet even so I don't think I could ever take flying the Atlantic seriously. Keep a straight compass course, and, provided the engines don't fail, you've got to hit land somewhere.'

The mechanics pulled the chocks away, and we headed out to sea. It was mid-July: there were icebergs below us and Northern Lights above us, but even at 10,000 feet it was warm enough to fly in shirtsleeves. We flew on and on: on through the daylight: on through the night and on to daylight once more. Nothing happened, and nothing went awry. The weather grew gradually worse, but the navigator and the wireless operator, young as they were, did their job perfectly, and ten and a half hours after take-off we hit the English coast three miles south of track.

CHAPTER TEN

BERLIN

As the taxi drew up outside the mess, Revs' long legs showed themselves through the window, straddling the porch.

'Gee, Revs, but it's good to see you! It seems so long.'

'Funny thing, I was just thinking of you. What sort of trip did you have?'

'Fine; a bit monotonous, except for the icebergs and the Northern Lights.'

'Did you bring a Liberator?'

'No, they wouldn't trust me with one. In fact they said I was only fit to be a second pilot. I must be worse than I thought I was. Still, they did break down in the end, under pressure: taught me to fly and to navigate all over again and packed me off in a Hudson.'

'Tell me about your wife. You gave us a shock when it came out in the papers.'

'I'm not good at describing people: you'd better wait till you meet her. Now tell me your news; it was quite like a reception committee seeing you standing here.'

'I wish there were more to meet you.'

'Who?'

'All the crew. Every single one except me.'

'But the C.O. promised they would be given a rest until I got back. They needed it: at least Taffy and Jacko certainly did.'

'I know, but there you are. The very last thing Taffy said as I saw him off was, "When's Mr. C. coming back?" He wasn't happy with his new captain.'

'Any news?'

'No, they were over Frankfurt. Hares wasn't with them: he went with Robby in the daylight over Kiel, and was definitely killed. The aircraft went into a vertical dive right on to the deck, followed by a 110, and Hares was firing right up to the last moment.'

'Just like him: you should have heard him when a fighter attacked us over the North Sea.'

'Jerry wasn't with them either: he went on to Fortresses and was killed in a crash.'

'Come on: let's go inside and have a drink.'

'Christopher's been doing magnificently. He's on Halifaxes too.'

'Yes, I heard. They gave him a staff job at Command, but he wouldn't have it. I'll give him a ring. Well, Revs, don't let ghosts walk, it's no use, and here's to the future.'

Next day they gave me a crew and an aircraft, but Revs was not included: why not we failed to discover: just one of those things. Instead he went off in a daylight attack against the *Scharnhorst* at La Pallice. As they were leaving the target, two fighters circled round him waiting to close. He happened to look down towards the sea and saw a third climbing straight up at him. From the way it was coming in it was obvious that it was going to be either the fighter or Revs, so Revs left the two above him. The fighter opened up at 600 yards and Revs held his fire to 400. The fighter came in and in and in, until at 50 yards he turned over on his back and went down in flames, but his fire had been accurate. The rear turret was riddled with holes, none of them further than two feet from Revs, and the wireless operator was killed. He had been leaning over the window, dancing with excitement at the sight of the battleship, when suddenly a look of utter, blank amazement spread over his face, and he said quietly: 'They've got me.'

Instead of Revs I had Martin, a wiry bus conductor from Tunbridge Wells, and therefore full of bright remarks at curious moments. He had only done three trips, but already could boast a D.F.M. Forty miles from Hanover; they were flying 200 feet or so above cloud, when a fighter emerged suddenly right behind them. The moment it broke cloud it opened fire, and its first burst put the starboard inner engine out of action and jammed the rear turret. The gun-sight was blown off, the intercom was gone, and Martin was wounded in his eye and arm. Although he could not operate the turret and therefore could only fire when the fighter came in from astern, he managed to drive it off. So much for the rear gunner: a good substitute.

Then there was Jock, once a Customs official from Leith, now a wireless operator with the experience of thirty-four trips. When people asked me what my wireless op was like, I said, 'Double Scotch and no water'. To counterbalance him, we had an Irishman: Paddy, from Londonderry; as yet no trips to his credit, but six years' service in the R.A.F. – an engineer, the fellow who understands all the knobs. In the nose, the coldest place of all, was Crock. Tall, crinkly dark hair, and good-looking, from London town. Once he knew all about leather; now, when he wasn't flying in the front turret or working on the wireless set, he had the job of blacking-out the windows, mounting the fore guns and pouring out coffee: anything, in fact, which the others were too lazy to do for themselves, but he always had a smile and a joke. On off days you would see him marching out in spotless uniform to meet his girl friend.

Second pilot was Stead. Young and fair and, until you grew to know him, shy, but nothing violent seemed to bother him. Before the war he was studying to be a vet. Then, most important of all, there was Henry, the navigator. He was a friend of Taffy's and I had known him in the early summer of 1940. Six days after war had been declared he was forced down in Belgium and interned, first of all in police headquarters in Brussels and then in a fort in Antwerp. The fort was well defended by a series of ditches, moats and rows of barbed wire, and so he remained there until the Germans invaded. After many days of walking and hitch-hiking and camping in the open he reached Boulogne, and crossed to England on the Isle of Man packet. The captain was not so fortunate; he escaped early on, rejoined the Squadron, was shot down over Holland and captured by the Germans. He escaped a second time, and reached St. Malo, but his ship was torpedoed, and not being able to swim he was drowned.

The night after we were crewed up, and before we had time to get used to ourselves we were sent to Berlin. It was the first raid of the season and therefore the defences were not prepared, which, as it happened, was just as well, because of the four aircraft scheduled to be there at the same time three failed to take off and the fourth was shot down on the way. It was a curious sensation being over Berlin alone, and we were glad to escape with only a few holes. That was the start, and so on it went. Berlin, Cologne, Berlin, Duisburg, Berlin, Essen and again Berlin. All of it routine and most of it unexciting.

Winter began to show her traces, and the Germans began to demonstrate what store they set by ground defence. The guns, it is true, were much the same as ever, a little more powerful and a little more accurate, but where there used to be one, there were now two, three, four and in places even ten. And as for the searchlights, the change was remarkable. Once they had been ineffective at 8,000 feet, now they were effective as high as 18,000. I have never flown as high as that, so I rely on someone else's word, but at least they held us at 11,000 feet over Berlin. And this is only half the story: where before there were fifty or sixty, there were now two or three hundred, and on a front reaching from Denmark right down south of Abbeville and stretching many miles inland; where once we had gambolled around in utter freedom, there was a festering bed, not of dozens or hundreds, but, whether you like it or not, of thousands. Yes, night bombing was indeed very different from what it had been eighteen months ago: night fighters, and a continuous barrier of shells and searchlights, and, more aggravating still, a host of knobs and technical instruments which we would have scorned in summer 1940. But, in spite of all this, the trips were no more interesting than before, nor were they any more exciting. For the simple reason that the work was no longer a novelty, and that more technical skill was required; the first carefree, exultant joy was, perhaps, gone, but in its place appeared an atmosphere of quiet enjoyment.

This quiet enjoyment, tempered by the recognition of a more dangerous enemy, was heightened by a few amusing incidents.

Willy arrived back safely from Montreal and embarked

upon a ferocious career of operations, and best of all, Jimmy came to join us. That was more than I had ever dared hope for. And Jimmy, once started, waged a veritable Blitzkrieg of his own: in fact, once he did three trips in two days.

One night, on the way back from Berlin, we ran short of petrol. Paddy suddenly chirped up as we were crossing the coast:

'I think you'd better land straight away, Captain: the tanks are reading more or less zero.'

'Nuts, Paddy. Last time we went to Berlin they told us we had 190 gallons left. The weather's been bad, I admit, and we've been longer in the air, so we won't have that amount on board, but none the less we've got plenty. The gauges must be U.S. Anyway, I want to go to town this afternoon, and I'm getting back by hook or by crook.'

However, Paddy would not have it, and five minutes later the port outer motor cut.

'Balance cock on, Engineer. She ought to pick up if you're quick.'

'O.K., sir,' and Paddy dashed down the fuselage to the cocks.

'What are you going to do now? The others may cut any minute, and there's forty miles to go. We're over hills too, and not much to spare.'

'To hell with you.'

'Do you want a bearing, Captain?'

'No, it's O.K. I'm on the beam.'

But the engine did not pick up, and just as the aerodrome lights came into view the starboard outer cut too. The flare-path was dead ahead: whether we were into wind or not I was going to land, and, as it happened, we were into wind – perhaps Desmond was right after all, with his cesspit, gold watch and chain idea. There was a Whitley landing just in front. I flashed the lights and came in beside him, just on his starboard. The flarepath gave us red after red – just to make it more difficult – and someone shrieked at us on R/T, but we ignored all protests and bobbed down safely, Paddy saying the meantime: 'I told you so, Captain.'

The same week, as we were flying down England towards

Cologne, there was a sudden rattle of machine-guns from just behind my back. I came to life with a start and hurtled down into a cloud, pitching Stead off his perch.

'Where the hell did that come from?'

'It's only Crock, sir.'

'Only!'

'Yes, I think he's shot himself through the foot.'

'Don't be a bloody fool!'

'Here, come off it, Cocky; I'm not a blinking camel. Captain, tell him to stop it.'

'Who's that speaking?'

'Rear gunner here.'

'Yes, Martin, what's the trouble?'

'Second wireless op's just shot my thermos flask away.'

'Come on, Martin, pull yourself together; he's not a blacksmith, you know, and bullets don't come out of a gun and then whistle off at right-angles. Engineer, go and see what's going on.'

'Crock says he was swinging the guns out of the window when he slipped and pulled the trigger by mistake. He managed to miss his foot all right, but he nearly got Martin.'

'Crock, you're not to do it. You've got to be polite to Martin as long as you're both in the same aeroplane, even if you don't like him.'

'Okidoke, Captain: I'll give him a pint of beer when we land. Pity about his thermos flask, though; they haven't got any more in stores.'

When we came back there was fog over the aerodrome, so we were diverted further north. As I walked into interrogation, Christopher was there before me, looking very well and cheerful. I had not seen him since the eve of my departure for the New World. He said – well, what does it matter what he said? Because we talked for a long time, both of us, and, being brothers, our conversation would seem to anyone else somewhat sentimental.

Skip, the interrogation officer, shouted out:

'Did you hit the target?'

'No.'

'Your brother did.' There was a touch of pride in his voice.

'Damned line-shooter: he was just kidding.'

'He's got a photograph to prove it. I suppose the camera's kidding too. What height did you come down to?'

'Nine thousand.'

'Your brother came down to 7,500.'

'O.K., Skip, the younger generation seems to be pushing you and me into the background.'

Skip put his arm on my shoulder and said: 'This is the fourth time you two have been over the same target at the same time. Keep it going, lad, you've created a record already.'

Next Tuesday we scored four direct hits on the Gelsenkirchen hydrogen plant, and there were a series of vast, blue-green explosions. Christopher was there too; and the very next night was the most successful trip of all.

Karlsruhe. As usual a quiet route. A few shells over the French coast, accuracy hopeless, but maybe they weren't firing at us. Anyway, I did not bother to take evasive action. Patches of cumulonimbus to 10,000 feet: about 8/10ths: we flew just above them. I saw the coast for an instant and recognized Dunkirk – fifteen miles to starboard of track. Henry was able to work out the wind and ten minutes later gave me an alteration of course. Some searchlights round Charleroi: a fighter – looked like an Me.109 – came up to look at us, but decided not to attack. Quarter of an hour before E.T.A. a bunch of searchlights and A.A. appeared ahead and to port. From the map it should be Mannheim, but there was nothing coming up from where Karlsruhe ought to be and I did not know that anyone was attacking Mannheim, so I decided to go in and make certain – quicker than getting a pin-point on the intermediate stages of the river.

Yes, it was Mannheim all right: we recognized the peculiar Y shape of the river to the north of the town. The clouds were awkward – base 11,000 feet, which gave the searchlights a good background. Went in at 10,000 feet and the master light got us straight away: the rest got us too, plenty of them. I tried for a moment to break out but could not do it, so I put the nose down, full boost, and headed up-river for Karlsruhe – no use giving the guns more time to shoot by twisting and turning about, and the defences were not so very wide. The A.A. started up pretty soon: most of it could not get our speed, but some was accurate and made plenty of noise. Paddy shouted something about being caught in searchlights; after all, he was a bit lonesome down by the flare-chute.

'Cut it out, Paddy. The lights can't hurt us and the guns are way behind us.'

At least it sounded quite good, but the next two shots were very close – much too close – and made me jump.

'Ack-ack behind: better get weaving, Captain.'

This was Martin, of course, in his inimitable fashion.

'O.K., here we go, flying down the river – to Rio.'

Paddy laughed, and Jock, not quite understanding what was going on but refusing to be outdone, extricated his head from his wireless set and burst into some wild Gaelic melody. And so, to the tune of his fading cries, we waltzed out of Mannheim at 4,000 feet.

Karlsruhe loomed up unexpectedly – I must have underestimated our speed – and what a sight it was too: three guns, five searchlights and four large fires burning away, almost apologetically. We came down to 6,000 feet, identified the target and opened the bomb-doors. Henry said he felt sorry for the place and could not bring himself to drop the bombs, but then he is apt to be an insincere sort of fellow and you can't always trust him. He certainly did not look sorry when the bombs burst where they should have done, and the roof of the locomotive factory came up to meet the sky. We circled round for a while taking photographs and watching the fire grow larger and larger, then we set course for home. Martin broke unexpectedly into conversation to say frivolously he had seen the sights on the three guns.

The return journey was uneventful: we saw another fighter and a Wellington: searchlights not troublesome and a few more belated shots from Dunkirk. At Base the weather was perfect: in fact, everything was perfect. We were third man home and found we had a beautiful photograph.

On the strength of it I bought the most adorable French poodle puppy in the world. It came from that heavenly hound-shop behind Berkeley Square; unblushingly left its mark on the 'Mayfair''s best carpet, and had bestowed upon it the name 'Simon'. Jock, Henry and Crock were there too, so I left them to look after Simon and went off to cable Constance.

When I came back, Jock was not alone. He said he had never had so many beautiful girls come up to him in all his life, and figured out that the passport to success was to buy a poodle puppy. Alf – you know Alf, the non-stop smiling bartender of the 'Mayfair'? – grinned all over his face and said: 'Look here, next time you go over, you drop 'em a good big 'un from me: right in the knobbly middle of their knobbly bones. That will give 'em *Ersatz*,' and licking his chops at the thought he stood us all a drink, God bless his soul.

News: and I mean real news. Taffy, Jacko, Brown and Gutteridge all safe, the only casualty being Jacko, who broke his leg.

'Shall I lay the track off to Borkum and then straight to target, sir?'

'No, Henry, certainly not!'

'But we've been routed that way.'

'I don't care how we've been routed, and I don't care who routed us. I don't care if I have to be court-martialled when we get back: I am not going via Borkum. If you go a little to port of track you fly slap over Bremen and Emden, to starboard you hit Wilhelmshaven and Hamburg, and if you keep dead on track you get shot to hell by the defended belt. No, Henry, it may have been the right way last month, but tonight it definitely is not. Call it a hunch or anything you like, but you'll see I'm right when we get there. Anyway, the only thing I believe about guns is what I see with my eyes, not what I'm told, and since it's our lives in the balance, I think we'll trust our own eyes.'

'Which way are you going then? North?'

'No, south: right south, as near to Hanover as we can get. We won't get a shot fired at us that way, and the clouds are far too thick for searchlights. What the hell we're going for anyway I can't think: fronts all the way and icing and

10/10ths cloud everywhere: we haven't a hope of seeing anything. Somehow I've a shrewd suspicion the Russians are going to be there, too, but the peculiar thing is that for the first time in my life I don't want to go: I'd much rather have a glass of beer and go to bed. Awful thing to admit, but still, there you are. I guess it's just the weather that's so bad.'

'We'll have to climb to 15,000 to clear the cold front.'

'Yes, I know. I hope it's not too cold. I'm going to leave you now, Henry: I think I'll go and ring my brother and find out what route he's taking. See you later.'

The Flight Commander called me into his office.

'Oh, I've something to tell you.'

'Yes, sir?'

'You're going missing tonight.'

'Who sold you that story?'

'Just a premonition, but my premonitions are always right.'

'This one isn't.'

'I want Simon. I love puppies. I'll look after him until you get back – if you ever do. Will you sign a statement saying I can have him?'

'I'll sign anything you like, but it won't do you any good.'

'Well, will you sign?'

'No; as it happens, I won't. Meanwhile I've got to go and change.'

I was glad I was flying now, but I did not succeed in getting through to Christopher.

The trip was much as I expected: everywhere these towering, billowing heap-clouds, and, as Henry forecast, we had to climb to 15,000 feet to avoid them. On our port, all the way across Germany, the sky was infested with shells, but, as it happened, only once or twice did we have a burst aimed at us. Instead a few searchlights circled round us ineffectively, and a fighter hovered indecisively on our tail before finally making off. It was cold, damn it, and the clouds would not let us come down into warmer air. Henry said map-reading was hopeless, so we fell back on Jock and his bearings.

'Have a look at the oxygen connections, will you, Paddy?

It's vanishing pretty rapidly, and we don't seem to be getting much value for our money.'

Hanover came and trickled past, away on our starboard, and not a shot to disturb us. Stead thought the searchlights looked very bright, and Paddy went back to change over tanks.

Over to port, round Bremen and Wilhelmshaven, the ack-ack never ceased.

'Crikey, Captain, these Germans put some stuff into the air, don't they? Don't they ever run out of ammunition or anything?'

And I took some gentle evasive action as a few guns opened up beneath us. The clouds began to break very gradually, and overhead the stars winked, as if amused.

'My bottom's getting sore, Captain. Can't you shove on an extra ten miles an hour?'

'Quiet, Crock, or I'll make you go and man the beam guns. It's cold down there.'

Then, some time later, a line of twinkling lights appeared low on the horizon ahead of us. Berlin, or at least the outer defences. I shifted in my seat and looked at the temperature gauge – 19°C.: not so bad, but none the less bad enough; I might have brought a flying-suit really. Gradually the lights rose higher and higher, and gradually, too, they grew larger and more orange.

I thought: 'Well, that proves the earth is round, doesn't it?'

Slightly to port, and well ahead, like a monstrous fire in the distance, came the moon. Height 13,500 feet, and round about a few more breaks in the cloud. Suddenly, like a jack-in-the-box, the searchlights sprang up, and started upon their tortuous course through the heavens. The big guns – 4·7s, and perhaps even larger – came slowly closer until finally they were right beneath.

'E.T.A. seventeen minutes.'

'Blimey, these defences must be pretty wide.'

At last, after two hours over enemy territory, we heard the familiar *woomph* of the shells: quite like home again, but after half an hour we all decided we could have done without it.

'This is murderous, isn't it? And it doesn't matter which way you turn, it seems to stretch for miles and miles. I think we'll drop the bombs here.'

'That's the sixth time you've said that, Captain. For heaven's sake let's drop them and get out of here: it isn't healthy flying round like this, and you can't possibly see anything because of all the clouds.'

'I know, Martin, that's just how I feel myself, but it's awful to come all this way and then go and bomb an open field. I'll fly over and have a look at that flare away to port.'

As it happened we looked at many flares, but none of them seemed to help us very much.

'Look at that! It's pitiful to watch it. I wish to God he'd put his nose down and dive out of it or something: it's only a matter of seconds now if he keeps on at the same height.'

It lasted two minutes exactly, and then, as was bound to be, he burst into flames. He was dead at our height, and less than half a mile away. As the flames broke out, most of the guns closed down, but some of them – twenty or thirty or so – went on firing, and their shells were bursting right among the wreckage.

'I hope to God it's not Christopher.'

'No, sir, it looked more like a Wellington than a Halifax.'

'Thanks, Jock, for those few words, but I know damn' well you couldn't tell the difference from here.'

Fifty-five minutes we were under fire, and then we left the defences behind. As on the way in, the route was free from guns, but away on the starboard the barrage never ceased, and all around the clouds were menacing. Twelve thousand feet: what a height to bomb from! Lofty and Desmond and Hares and the rest, they had never been up that high, but perhaps they would understand.

First of all came memories of those old days: of Desmond imitating the Irish, and walking round the aerodrome, his hands clasped behind his back, and Pluto, the faithful bloodhound, snuffling along beside him. Lofty, too, towering above the world and flicking me under the chin; and Jimmy, when snow first appeared on the Yorkshire hills, saying:

'Gee, but that can't be snow: there isn't any on Lofty's head.'

And then the memories became misty and cloudy. Cloudy: yes, everywhere round here is cloudy. Martin reported a fighter on his tail, so we disappeared into a cloud. Wonderful friends, these clouds, at times, but somehow feathery and almost unreal. The moon was higher and her reflection showed silver tinged with grey around and beside us. My mind slipped further and further away until it was miles and miles up in the ether and its only earthbound link the roar of the motors. I saw visions of Lofty and Desmond and other, smaller figures, flitting in and out of the clouds, laughing, hovering around, as if a barrier between danger and us. Well, who knows? Men like Lofty and Desmond don't die. The visions became clearer and less general. I saw a boyish figure – no one in particular, just a boy – but somehow he represented all the men who had meant so much in the past. He was up among the clouds in a world that you and I don't know, but a world one day we will know, and none the less a human figure just like you or I. He was a young boy and he was going somewhere. Where, I could not quite make out: perhaps down to earth, because clearly it was some place he knew nothing about, and because of that he was very, very frightened. There were a lot of other boys with him, and they were frightened too, just as he was, but somehow he was more shy and more backward than they. Then I noticed something else. There was a woman among them, a very beautiful and majestic woman. They all seemed to be in love with her, to be fighting among themselves to win her, and that was why the small boy was so frightened. He did not think he could win her; no, that was impossible, he was too backward and shy, but at least he wanted to see her, to be able to speak to her, and he thought that he would never see her again. Perhaps it was that they were all going to take a test and that only the winner would come back to her. The small boy fell at her knees and poured out his soul. She looked at him and said slowly and very quietly:

'Once you have gone you will forget all about me, and you

will pray day and night that the time of your returning may be as far off as possible.'

And so with that he went.

For a time things were blurred, and then war broke out. Still the same shy, frightened boy, he joined up, not because he wanted to fight, but because a few important men made a lot of impressive speeches telling him that it was his duty. He did not know that, had these men so wished, there would never have been any war, but perhaps that was just as well. As he marched along to the front he passed a preacher on a soap-box – 'Peace and Goodwill be among men' he was saying. 'God has given you life to do what you wish with it: why therefore do you bend yourself to the will of others who have only been seeking their own advancement?'

The boy thought of the home and the quiet he had left behind him, but he went on marching. Before he had been at the front many days his platoon was sent forward to destroy a bridge before the enemy could reach it. He was afraid now: more afraid than he had ever been, for he was young, and there were so many things he wanted to do before he died. So he found himself falling behind the others, and because he was behind he was only wounded by the shell that killed the rest of them. Somewhere through his mind there ran a phrase he had heard before: 'Peace and Goodwill be among men.' He might have stayed and lived, honourably too: but instead he went on. It was not easy, but he did it, and he blew the bridge up – but himself with it.

The plane hit a bump and jerked me, but before I woke up I saw a final fleeting vision. The scene was once more among the clouds, but this time the boy and the woman were alone, and this time the boy had grown into the splendour of maturity, and, instead of kneeling at the woman's feet, she was kneeling at his. She said: 'You see, I told you you would dread coming back to me, but you conquered that dread, and if it had not been for that it would not have been worth while going at all.'

I think he must have passed the test.

Revs met us as we climbed out of the plane.

'What sort of a trip did you have?'

'Pretty lousy on the whole, the weather was hopeless. Apart from cloud all the way, the ground was thick with haze.'

'Much ack-ack?'

'Yes, plenty, but we got off pretty lightly: a few holes, that's all. Somebody must have caught it, though; we saw four aircraft go down in flames, and I don't believe they were Germans.'

'The Russians were over there too.'

'I had a hunch they would be. I'm glad to be down, Revs; I've had a creepy feeling up my spine all night, and for some unknown reason it's still there.'

'Come and have some coffee.'

'Yes, but just a moment. I want to go to Ops. Room.'

Interrogation was over; dawn was just breaking, but it was bleak, not at all what an autumn morning should be. I knocked on the door and found Smith on duty by the telephone.

'Ring up seventy-six for me and find out whether my brother's down safely, will you, please?'

He flicked a switch and turned a handle and spoke into the microphone, but his face showed blank.

'They say they're very busy getting a stray aircraft home and we'll have to ring later.'

So that was it. I knew the night had boded no good.

CHAPTER ELEVEN

CONCLUSION

The days turned into weeks, and still no news of Christopher, not even an indication of what had happened. Two nights after he was shot down I nearly followed suit.

Magdeburg. As far as Hanover it was clear as could be and the moon was up, but from then on came the usual unceasing cloud. On E.T.A. we felt certain of our position and therefore decided to come down and look for clearer air. The guns opened up, and, in spite of the cloud, were exceptionally accurate. I feathered all four airscrews, switched the motors off, and turned through 180°. It was a curious sensation watching a row of dead props over Germany, but none the less it fooled the defences completely: they continued firing way behind us along our previous course and then finally stopped altogether. At 9,000 feet, for safety's sake, I tried to restart one engine, just to see if everything was in order, but everything was not in order: it refused to pick up. I called Paddy back from the fuselage and we got to work. Feathering knobs, starter buttons, magneto switches, throttles and airscrew pitch controls, all at the same time. It must have been a funny sight watching us, but nothing very much happened. The engines turned over slowly and even fired for a brief moment, but that was all. At 7,000 feet the starboard outer started and of course the ack-ack opened up immediately. What we really wanted was the inboards, because they worked the generators, and the batteries could not last much longer under this strain. At 5,000 feet the starboard inner started: both on the same side; with bombs on we could not maintain height. One of the port engines kept bursting into life and then stopping again. At 4,000 feet we jettisoned the bombs.

What with the roar of shells and the crackling of the

intercom and looking round at everything, trying to make out which engine really was running, it was difficult to know what was happening, but at least the bombs fell in the middle of Magdeburg's defences. Shortly afterwards a heavy burst hit us underneath the port wing and threw us into a spin or a dive – I could not make out which. The instruments must have hit the stops, for they went out of action completely, except for the altimeters, which still showed a rapid rate of descent. The controls locked hard over in the starboard position and nothing that I could do would move them. The instruments showed no signs of recovering and amid all the ack-ack we were still going down: we could not be more than 2,000 feet from the ground.

'The aircraft's no longer under control; you'll have to jump . . . Jump!'

But nobody moved from their seat. Crock, though we did not know it then, was standing in the fuselage without a helmet and oblivious of what was going on.

'Come on, Ches, you can do better than that. Come on, sir, we trust you. Pull us out of it: you've come out of worse holes than this. Come on, sir.'

'Yes, Jock, I think I can.'

I realized then what had happened. The shell-burst had thrown us on our side, and simultaneously both port motors had started, forcing us further and further over. I throttled them back quickly, and we returned to normal. As we broke cloud, six fighters in close formation flashed by, but they did not attack.

The weeks went by, and the succeeding trips grew less eventful. Jimmy was shot down over Berlin, and I thought: 'Well, really, this is too much.' I had been through everything, even America, with Jimmy; somehow I could not believe he would ever go. He was too strong, too cheerful, to go the way of the others; but then that's no criterion. I thought back nine months ago to Christmas Day when he had kissed the W.A.A.F.s under the mistletoe and Lofty and Desmond and Lousy and Frammy and Lib and Jimmy and I had drunk to the future. Every one of them dead, and now

Jimmy gone, too. Willy wandered round for three days saying: 'That shakes your confidence completely: if a man like Jimmy goes, anybody can go.' And then he went missing himself.

I wrote letters to every Government Department in London trying to get permission for Constance to come to England, but they all said they were too busy and could not be bothered. I went to the Foreign Office and asked them to cable New York to the effect that I was a British subject. They packed me off to the Passport Control Office, and from there I was sent back to the Foreign Office. Eventually Air Ministry came to my rescue. On Tuesday, September 2nd, no cable arrived from New York, but it was all right: three turned up next day.

One morning, round lunch-time, came the news I had been waiting for so long. Christopher was safe. What wild rejoicing there was that day, and what a weight off my heart! Willy was safe too, in the same camp, but Jimmy was dead. So life was not so good after all. Of the old days, that wonderful summer and winter of 1940, everybody was gone except Revs, and he was not allowed to fly with me. I flew up to Orkneys to bring the C.-in-C. back, and walked down to the beach, because there would be the water that was bringing Constance nearer every minute. But I was wrong. For the third time they had cancelled her sailing.

Then came a letter from Christopher – safe and sound. And soon after his engineer wrote describing what had actually happened. 'We were flying fairly high through a barrage of A.A. fire, when a group of searchlights caught and held us. We tried to get out of them, but found we could not. Things were getting bad, and to settle everything, an explosive shell burst on the tail wheel, which set the machine uncontrollable and a deathly silence from the tail gunner. The machine started into an ever-increasing dive, when the captain gave the order to jump. The wireless operator and observer and second pilot jumped in turn; the captain happened to be at the next escape hatch, with me very close behind. By this time the machine was diving steeply and the captain, regardless of himself, stepped over the hatch and let me go first, which I did. The rest of the crew landed safely by 'chute, but I regret we presume both tail gunner and front gunner dead, because we had not seen or heard anything of them. We think the tail gunner was killed by the explosive shell and the front gunner had not time to get out.'

I thought back for the hundredth time on that trip to Berlin and wondered where all this had happened and how far away I was at the time. But speculation yielded no results, so I offered up a silent vote of admiration and left it. What a difference it makes to life to have a brother to be proud of!

A few days later came my third wartime birthday, and with it many startling developments. Revs at last joined me. The weather was perfect, the target was Berlin and the moon was full. Who could ask for a finer set of circumstances? We landed back in the early light of dawn with the moon still light in the sky, and Revs, as had been his wont in the past, carried my 'chute out of the aeroplane. He set his jaw at an angle, clamped his teeth on his pipe, and smiled contentedly, like a cow.

'Magnificent, Leonard. Magnificent. The best trip I have ever done.'

'Yes, Revs, life's just starting. But I never thought I'd live to see Berlin as clearly as that.'

'It's the first time I've heard you sing down the intercom since last December. What were you circling round for after dropping the bombs?'

'I lived in Berlin once for four months, with Admiral von Reuter; I was looking for his house.'

'Did you find it?'

'No, but I saw the street: right by the Potsdam Lake. It stands out quite well.'

'Tell me, you remember on the way back, somewhere near Lübeck, a battery of guns opened up, and almost immediately you put the aircraft down in a screaming dive. What made you do that? I've never known you act that way before.'

'I don't know at all. I had been flying along half asleep for some time dreaming about something or other – probably wondering whether we were going to see another fighter – when I saw the flashes on the ground, and the next thing I knew we were on our nose. I didn't seem to do it: it just happened.'

'Just as well, because they only missed us by a few yards as it was, and there was plenty of them.'

'Yes, I know. H'ya, Jim boy. I'm sorry: I mean good morning, sir.'

'Good trip?'

'Wizard!'

'You are off ops.'

'What did you say?'

'You've been taken off ops.: you're through, finished, grounded.'

'Yes, all right, I heard you. What's the trouble?'

'Nothing. You're through, that's all.'

We sat down at the table, all seven of us, and the Colonel asked us the usual routine questions. I looked around me at the six faces and thought: 'From now on I'm just another has-been, from now on I've got to sit in the background and live on memories, because never again will I be able to capture the companionship and confidence of men like these around me.' I shook them by the hand and walked out.

'How do you feel?'

'I don't know, Revs: how does one feel when a career is suddenly snatched away? It's like having a limb cut off.'

'It's not so bad really: you'll come back one of these days.'

'Yes, I know. I suppose I'll get used to it in time, but at the moment it hurts. It's like someone kicking you in the pants and saying: "We've had enough of you, get out."'

'What are you going to do?'

'Right now? I'm going to be sick.'

I was, too, right in front of the guard.

'I'll go and get you some bicarb.'

'No, it's not that: my stomach's like leather. Come on, let's go and have a glass of beer, like Lofty used to. I was just thinking.'

'What?'

'We consider ourselves pretty tough flying over Germany under cover of darkness of vast heights, but what about these Blenheim and Coastal Command boys who come over in broad daylight at zero feet and think nothing of it. Makes you think, doesn't it? Hullo, there's a cable. Good lord, look at this!'

'What is it?'

'Constance, from Canada: "This is hello, darling. Am wearing furs. All love." She's on her way: I can hardly believe it. You know, there's something I have to thank this war for; something I value far, far above any glory or success, or even memories. Once – not very long ago – I found something I wanted more than anything else in the world, but the matter was not very simple. People I knew screamed at me and said: "For God's sake wait, man; you've only known her three weeks; if you've got to do it, give yourself time and make certain you are sure of yourself." Well, I might easily have given in to them – after all, they were more experienced than I, and defying people you've known all your life is quite a large break – but I didn't, I took the bit in my teeth and got married on the spot, only just in time. If I hadn't I should have been too late, and now I should be an embittered specimen of humanity despising myself for having no guts, and hating everybody who managed to influence me. And so, to be egotistical, that is what these few operations have done for me. They have taught me that when you get something you really want, you've got to hang on to it at all costs, because if you once let it go you'll never get another chance.'

EPILOGUE

At ten-five the first Whitley passed over the aerodrome heading south-east, and at eleven-twenty the port outer of 'E' for Edward roared into life. It had roared into life countless times during the last seven months, but tonight there was something different, something that spelt success and, for that matter, death, and so it was that the routine look of boredom was gone from the six faces inside 'E' for Edward. Gone was the sun, but the sky was still light enough to see the host of bombers floating irresistibly towards Cologne. From the control tower someone flashed a green, and we fled down the flarepath to take our place in the queue: behind us, dimly, we saw the departure of 'N' for Nuts, and then the night closed down. The faces beside me were unfamiliar, but the spirit was the same as ever. I had wondered if it would feel different, starting again: I wondered too if the sight of gunfire would frighten me, or if the absence of the old, trusted faces would take away the confidence I once had known. All this, and more, I had asked myself during the hours of preparation, and then, when the night closed in and the flarepath disappeared behind the port wing, I knew that the answer was No. I realized in that moment that the Air Force has achieved something greater than all its victories, that through the wisdom and courage of its leaders it has created among its ranks a fellowship which can never be destroyed; and I think I understood why it is that England can never be defeated.

As we flew on across England, in the sky and on the ground there were signs of inexhaustible activity: flarepaths, aeroplanes and lights pointing out the way. Aeroplanes over the sea, too, and ships patrolling in case of accidents. And then as we turned over the Dutch islands on to the last lap, the most monstrous sight in all the history of bombing. The sky, helped by the moon, was very light, so that the stars showed only dimly and infrequently. The ground too was light, but in a curious manner mauve, so that the contrast was very beautiful. Against this pale, duck-egg blue and the greyish-mauve were silhouetted a number of small black shapes: all of them bombers, and all of them moving the same way. One hundred and thirty-four miles ahead, and directly in their path, stretched a crimson-red glow: Cologne was on fire. Already, only twenty-three minutes after the attack had started, Cologne was ablaze from end to end, and the main force of the attack was still to come. I looked at the other bombers, I looked at the row of selector switches in the bomb compartment, and I felt, perhaps, a slight chill in my heart. But the chill did not stay long: I saw other visions, visions of rape and murder and torture. And somewhere in the carpet of greyish-mauve was a tall, blue-eyed figure waiting behind barbed-wire walls for someone to bring him home. No, the chill did not last long.

I glued my eyes on the fire and watched it grow slowly larger. Of ack-ack there was not much, but the sky was filled with fighters. Every now and then we saw air-to-air tracer, and usually something would fall burning from the heavens: German or British? We could not tell which; only hope. In the tail and down the fuselage the gunners kept an even stricter watch; and all the time the fire grew larger and larger. Thirteen thousand feet below, the covering intruder force had swung into action, and against the venom of their machine-guns the German defences let fly to the winds the last vestige of concerted opposition. We watched the snuffing-out of searchlights and the strafing of aerodromes and said with thankfulness: 'Here at last is the first bomber battle, and the bombers are winning.'

When Cologne came in view beneath the port wing there was a sudden silence in the aeroplane. If what we saw below was true, Cologne was destroyed. We looked hastily at the Rhine, but there was no mistake: what we saw below was true. Cologne was burning, it was burning as no city in the world can ever have burnt, and with it was burning the morale of the German citizen.

Two nights later the Ruhr was burning too; not quite the same as Cologne, but none the less burning. In Cologne there was one fire as large as Hyde Park with fifty or sixty fires as large as the Ritz. In the Ruhr there were as many fires, but they were more widely dispersed. The visibility was worse, but none the less the Ruhr was burning, and for the second time the bombers had won the battle. We were scarred a little, perhaps a little frightened too, for the gun-fire and searchlights had been accurate, but as we pointed the nose towards home there was nothing but victory spelt before our eyes. We sped through the belt of fighters and tracer and watched the intruders shooting-up the defences. We sped across the fields of Holland at tree level. The night was clear and the air very warm, but not much was said, for we were full, each of us, with our own thoughts. We flew over Rotterdam so low that the bullets of the defenders passed through the tops of the wings and out through the underneath. And so with the memory of success we came home to bed.

In all forty-eight hours since we first took off, and in that short time two separate areas had been devastated, but that was only part of the story. As I pulled the bedclothes over my shoulders I felt a curious happiness inside my heart. For the first time in history the emphasis of night bombing had passed out of the hands of the pilots and into the hands of the organizers, and the organizers had proved their worth. In spite of the ridicule of some of their critics, they have proved their worth. They have proved, too, beyond any shadow of doubt that given the time the bomber can win the war. Not only have they proved it, they have written the proof on every face that saw Cologne and the Ruhr.